Also by Bhupinder Singh Mahal

Punjab: a Cataclysmic Showdown, Aftermath, and Challenges (2009)
Punjab: the Nomads and the Mavericks (2000)

The Making of the Sikh Empire

The role of Banda Bahadur and the Misls

By

Bhupinder Singh Mahal

S. Tallim & Co
2013

Copy right © Bhupinder Singh Mahal 2013
All rights reserved

ISBN 978-0-9686736-1-4

Jacket illustration (front): painting by I. Lynch of Dundas, Ontario

To my wife Suneeta
for her unshakeable
love and friendship

CONTENTS

Foreword

Preface

1. Introduction   1

2. Punjab: a hallowed land, an Eden lost   12

3. Evolution of warrior-saint culture   19

4. Banda Bahadur: the man, exploits and legacy   47

5. Idea of misl, evolution, and sphere of influence   71

6. Rise and fall of misls, intra and inter misl rivalries   81

    Bhangi   86
    Kanhaya   97
    Ramgarhia   103
    Singhapuria   112
    Karorasinghian   115
    Dhallewalian   120
    Nakkai   120
    Shaheedan   122
    Nishanwalia   123
    Ahluwalia   126
    Phulkian   132
    Sukerchakia   144

7. Sukerchakia juggernaut crushes all adversaries   163

8. Hegemony over Punjab - Afghans, Marathas
   & Sikh misls battle it out   173

9. Emergence of Sikh hegemony over Punjab   187

10. Epilogue   207

Glossary

Index

FOREWORD

In 2010 the celebration of the 300th anniversary of the establishment of first Sikh rule under Banda Singh Bahadur in 1710 created much interest in examining the legacy of his period. It prompted Bhupinder Singh Mahal to dig into eighteenth-century history of the Punjab, a subject of his fascination reflected in his earlier works -- Punjab: the Nomads and the Mavericks (2000) and Punjab: a Cataclysmic Showdown: Aftermath and Challenges (2009). In the present work he turns his gaze into the Sikh past about which competing views are available in different narratives. Recent scholarship maintains that historical facts do not lead to one story but interpretation of such facts to create various versions of the history and therefore 'critical histories'. I would like to make two observations right at the outset which must be kept in mind while reading Mahal's narrative.

First, one of the difficulties of understanding the story of eighteenth-century Sikh misls ('confederacies') is the paucity of contemporary sources. The traces of available evidence are scattered in Persian, Punjabi and some other languages. In particular, the Persian sources are highly prejudiced against the Sikhs. Sometimes, these sources are based on rumors about the personal lives of prominent Sikh leaders. Therefore, a caution is required for any objective analysis of these sources. Going through the present narrative one can easily recognize that it is based primarily on secondary sources in English language, not on the examination of original sources. Throughout his analysis, Mahal takes issue with Sikh historians to offer his views on the nature and function of Sikh misls.

Second, in order to understand contextual depth one might like to visit the geographical locations linked with the stories of the Sikh misls. Unfortunately, the boundaries of Punjab have been changing from time to time. Much of the geographical area related to Sikh misls is no longer part of Indian Punjab. It is no wonder that Mahal resents that "the areas that Sikh misls shed their blood to wrest control of from the Afghans, Marathas and the Moguls - including but not limited to Gujranwala, Sialkot Gujrat, Sargodha, Kasur, Pakpattan, Multan and Bahawalpur – are lost forever by being made an integral part of Pakistan."

Mahal's main focus is to look at severe factionalism among the misl chiefs who were driven by their own interests. They cooperated with each other only at the time of external aggression when their survival was at stake. He challenges the widely held notion of misls as nationalists or the architecture of Sikh empowerment and nation building. He does however maintains that the "Sikh misldars (supreme commanders) promoted the Khalsa creed with the result that Sikh peasants vacated their service to imperial agencies and threw their lot with the community and faith." These peasants formed the large pool of military recruitment for the misldars.

According to Mahal's narrative, the misl leaders neither owned nor ruled over any territory in Punjab. They had carved between themselves spheres of control, an area within which each misl was free to make forays to pillage. Therefore, to all intents and purposes they were engaged in plain banditry except that when the Sikh collectivity was in harm's way they would be summoned before the Sarbat Khalsa ('Entire Khalsa') at the Akal Takhat in Amritsar – the seat of temporal and religious authority among the Sikhs - to unite for a common purpose or against a common foe. This dual role made the misl leaders bandit-warriors.

Without going into further details, I would like to encourage the reader to understand Bhupinder Singh Mahal's take on the factional-ridden Sikh community in the eighteenth century. As a member of the Canadian Multiculturalism Advisory Committee, he has much experience to look at the Sikh issues from a much wider perspective. More recently, he has served as a Chairperson of an independent administrative tribunal that provides impartial quasi-judicial hearings on employment insurance decisions. It is no wonder that numerous awards and medals have recognized his role in Canadian cultural life.

In the end, I would like to commend this book to various readers. It offers a new angle to understand the eighteenth century Sikh history. It is written in an accessible and lucid style. It belongs in the library of scholars and lay people alike with an interest in Punjab studies.

Pashaura Singh
Professor and Dr. Jasbir Singh Saini Endowed Chair in Sikh and Punjabi Studies
Religious Studies Department, # 3050 INTN Bldg
University of California
900 University Avenue
Riverside, CA 92521

December 23, 2012

PREFACE

An article on Sikh misls published on Sikhchic was to rouse my interest.[1] The writer promoted the idea of organizing worldwide Sikhs along the lines of the 18th century misls e.g. Misl Amriki (American), Misl Angrezi (Great Britain). From what little I knew of the misls I was not sure they offered a good model to emulate.

Vaguely I recall two family historians tell me that one of our forebears was a sardar in the Singhpuria misl and how the misls lived on pillage; undermined one another; colluded with the enemy and so on.[2] That was my prompting to explore the misl period. More I read and researched, the more I became convinced the extent to which we have romanticized Banda Bahadur and the misl period.

For example, Gopal Singh asserts that Banda was the "first empire builder of the Sikhs"[3] while Patwant

---

[1] Sikh Misls, Part l: Yesterday, Today and Tomorrow by I.J. Singh published on Sikhchic.com -The Roundtable Open Forum #56 – on January 5, 2011

[2] Madhusudan Singh and Udham Singh, my father's cousins, are sons of Ujaggar Singh who wrote "The Antiquity of the Jat Race". Latter is my father's taya (uncle)

[3] History of the Sikh People by Gopal Singh – p.354

Singh contends that Banda and his men "had wrested extensive territories from the paramount power to establish the first ever independent Sikh state complete with its royal seal, its own coins and an administrative system".[4]

However, a perusal of their accounts will indicate that Banda confined his range of activities to the territories between Jamna River and Sutlej River. Even here, his forays were within a radius of 75 Km of the city of Ambala: (e.g. Sirhind 50 km northwest; Kaithal 75 Km southwest; Mustafabad 50 Km southeast; Shahabad 24 Km southeast and Sadhaura 65 Km east). The area encompassed by these towns and cities is a small fraction of the Malwa region. In reality, Banda strode across these towns and cities determined to wreak revenge upon them, resulting in "wanton destruction of life and property of Mogul officials and landowners".[5] He did not appoint satraps or establish military posts to secure any of these cities, a basic governing imperative. There is no evidence that Banda tinkered with the administrative system that was put in place by Akbar in 1602, which system remained intact and only undergo some tailoring under the British rule.

In arguing that "The misl period witnessed resistance led by the Sikhs against the invaders and built up (perhaps unconsciously) the notion that the Punjab would be better off if it were ruled by Punjabis rather

---

[4] The Sikhs by Patwant Singh – p.81
[5] A History of the Sikhs by Khushwant Singh – Vol. 1 p.118

than remain a part of the Kingdom of Kabul or the Mogul empire", Khushwant Singh has casually exaggerated the exploits of the misls.[6]

The misls was motley of interest groups, who for the main part freelanced on their own, only interacting, which was infrequent, when own survival were at stake. Unlike the Marathas who, in 1761, fought the Afghan invader Ahmad Shah Abdali at the battle of Panipat, determined to rid Punjab of the scourge, there is no similar resistance in the chronicles of the misls. Rather, the misls engaged in plundering the baggage of Abdali while he was homeward bound to Kabul. The idea of a Punjab ruled by Punjabis did not exist and even when Maharaja Ranjit Singh established the Sikh kingdom he did not make Punjabi the language of the court.

In 1745 Sikh Jathas (bands), who until then were freelancing independently from one another and engaged in seizing control of villages near their strongholds in the hills and forests, were merged into twenty-five cavalry units under the command of Nawab Kapur Singh.

Sikh historians in general agree that the Sikh Jathas (bands) and their next incarnation, the misls, comprised a band of highwaymen and marauders. Holed up in remote mountain and forest fastnesses for the most part, these bands periodically swooped down on the plains to loot and pillage. The rival

---

[6] A History of the Sikhs by Khushwant Singh – Vol. 1 p.183

gangs often pillaged the same village or town. In time, stronger misls offered villagers and townspeople protection (rakhi) in return for payment.

The notion of misls as nationalists or the architects of Sikh empowerment and nation building are a widely held opinion. An essential concomitant of nation building is allegiance to one flag, shared goals, and interests that encourage and assist the social, cultural, and economic well-being of the citizenry. Such was not the raison d'etre of the misls.

Their own interests governed the misls. Each carved out its own fiefdom with no inclination to found a polity. At best of times, they were scattered tribal oligarchies, autocratic and even despotic with not a hint of nationalist fervor.[7]

Of recent, a novel idea is gaining currency that the single most important entry requirement to the ranks of the misl was to be an Amritdhari (baptized Sikh).

The contention by some that to be a misldar a person had to satisfy the key criterion of being initiated an Amritdhari (baptized) is without merit. Phul, founder of the Phulkian misl, was not baptized nor any of his six sons. It was not until 1735 that Phul's grandson, Ala Singh, took the baptism from Kapur Singh.

---

[7] Nationalism is the claim that each ethnic (or religious) group feeling itself to be a nation has the right to independent existence, ruled by its own nationals and its own laws in its own territory – S. E. Finer (The History of Government; Vol. lll, p.1475)

Although Kapur Singh of Fyzullahpur baptized Jai Singh of the Kanhaya misl, there is no record indicating his two siblings, Jhanda Singh and Singha, misldars in their own right, took the amrit (i.e. initiated). Similarly, whereas Khushal Singh, founder of the Ramgarhia misl, received baptism from Banda Bahadur, no one has substantiated that Jassa Singh, who eventually took over the chieftainship of the misl, and his two brothers (Tara Singh and Mali Singh) were administered amrit.

The Amritdhari criterion appears to be a newly minted idea by baptized Sikhs. There is something amiss about their advocacy. Even a cursory glance would have revealed that the misldars were anything but ascetic. They flouted Khalsa code of conduct (baptismal vows) by robbing and pillaging people of their hard-earned goods; engaged in indiscriminate killing of citizenry; and, indulged, as some did, in binge drinking, sometimes with fatal consequences.[8]

It remains unclear how these misconceptions (nationalism) and distortions (Amritdhari stipulation) take root.

Bhupinder Singh Mahal
6 Golfview Cr., Dundas, Ontario, L9H 6V7

---

[8] Bhangi sardar Gulab Singh died circa 1800 of excessive drinking in Bhaseen

1. INTRODUCTION

Firebrands, revolutionaries, renegades, and outlaws of the days of yore have undergone a metamorphosis in just about every culture. People have mythologized them and made heroes of them. Historians choose facts from a pool of facts that they deem valuable to create a compelling cultural saga, turning rebels and outlaws into heroes. Thus, history is "an unending dialogue between the past and present", so argued Edward Hallett Carr.

Radicals and mavericks appear on world stage during civil or ethnic strife or oppressive governance, be it foreign or homegrown. Their charisma, bravado, masks, escapes, and their skirmishes with authority win the hearts of people who idolize the rebel even if legend and myth fail to jive with historical facts.

Every culture has made hero of its bygone renegades in just about every epoch. By some extraordinary alchemy, these otherwise ruthless and brutish leaders transform themselves to champion of the dispossessed, the poor and downtrodden masses. People identify with the fanciful narrative the renegade or the outlaw represents and not their misdeeds and crimes.

Take for example Pancho Villa. At age 16, he was a fugitive from justice. He took refuge in the mountains living among other bandits; and, in 1896, he became their leader. The gang stole cattle, commandeered trains, robbed money, harassed feudal landowners, and killed adversaries with disdain. He turned into a guerilla fighter during the revolutionary war, awarded 25,000-acre hacienda in Durango, and becoming a prosperous hacienda owner. The peons saw Pancho as an avenger of the poor, a Mexican Robin Hood, while others saw him as a bloodthirsty bandit. Today history remembers him as someone who helped dismantle the hacendado system, an agrarian reformer, a revolutionary, and a folk hero.

Sikh culture is no different. Regaled to the children from infancy are anecdotes of the rise of Sikh power in eighteenth century Punjab. The stories and exploits of Banda Bahadur, Sikh misls, and the Sikh empire at its zenith under Maharaja Ranjit Singh, passed down by word of mouth, endear them to children. The lavishly embellished stories and memories enthrall the child who keeps alive the romantic lore and saga and transmit it to the next generation.

Several historians have told the story of the rise and fall of the Sikh misls in English. Some have variously accounted for intra-misl (infighting) and inter-misl (shifting alliances, rivalry and warring factions) events. They have described the metamorphoses of freebooters (unruly Jathas) to nationalists (misls) who battled foreign invaders and domestic overlords to assert hegemony over Punjab. They have detailed the melding together of the misls into a unitary Sikh kingdom.

This treatise covers the period beginning with Banda Bahadur's entry into Punjab in 1709 and ending in 1811 when Ranjit Singh secured land between Jhelum and Sutlej Rivers and became the undisputed raja of Punjab. Although the Mogul rule was on the wane during this period Muslim historians and writers provide an ample chronicle of Sikh history. The Mogul emperors supported court historians and biographers.[9]

Some writers of this period have glossed over the misl period entirely. Take the case of Mountstuart Elphinstone (1779-1859) who joined the East India Company in 1795 and promoted to the diplomatic corps in 1801 and who reputedly refused the post of Governor-General of India. He provides a brief glimpse into the life and times of Banda Bahadur. He addresses the exploits of Banda Bahadur whose forces "broke from their retreat and overran the east of the Punjab". However, mostly he discusses the Maratha-Mogul fight for dominance of Punjab. He has inexplicably ignored the misl period in his two-

---

[9] Akbar encouraged men of letters and arts to produce books on history, biography and other subjects. A school of Indian historiography was founded and a large number of histories were written by eminent historians - The Mogul Empire by Ashirbadilal Srivastava – p. 217-218
Jahangir who succeeded Akbar was a highly educated and cultured prince. His memoirs titled *Tuzuk-i-Jahangiri* is a testimony to his extraordinary knowledge – p.285-286

volume History of India.[10] He acknowledges that in the times of emperor Bahadur Shah the Sikhs "were the rising into a nation, and in our times have attained considerable political influence among the states of India".[11] However, he does not expand the narrative, which is baffling considering the thirty-two years he spent in India and that, at the time of his writing, in 1806, he must have been aware Maharaja Ranjit Singh was the undisputed ruler of Punjab.

Another English writer, George Forster, an officer of the East India Company, who while having traveled through Punjab, in 1783, has also inexplicably ignored activities of the Sikh misldars in his travel book other than mention of his encounter with the Khalsa troops and wrote about their sense of fierce independence, dress, weaponry, and the Rakhi system.[12] How could the momentous changes taking place in Punjab in the decade from 1773 and 1783 escape his notice, a period that saw the growing political control and influence of Sikh misldars in Punjab. During that period the Bhangi and Dallewalian misldars ravaged

---

[10] The History of India by Hon. Mountstuart Elphinstone – written in 1806; 5th edition published in 1866 by John Murray
[11] Ibid – Book XII, Chapter 1, page 678
[12] A Journey from Bengal to England, Through the Northern part of India, Kashmire (sic) Afghanistan, and Persia and into Russia, by the Caspian Sea – printed for R. Faulder & son in 1798– page 303. The book is mostly a collection of letters written with a couple of other chapters (e.g. a chapter on Rohillas).

vast areas between Jamna River and Ganges River which so appalled the Mogul emperor Shah Alam ll that he agreed to a quid pro quo of allowing Sikhs to maintain their sphere of control in the Jamna-Ganges Doab in return for a specified yearly payoff. Moreover, in 1783, Sukerchakia and Kanhaya misldars fought a pitched battle in Achal, a village about 10 Km from Nabha, in which Gurbaksh Singh, son of the Kanhaya chieftain, was killed.

Some writers have paid scant attention to the misl period. For example, Patwant Singh offers no profile of individual misl and his mention of individual misls is limited to the role each misl played in the rise of Ranjit Singh (Chapter 3 - "Empire of the Sikhs").[13] J.D Cunningham offers a minimal portrayal, bordering on the cursory.[14]

Even among historians who have covered the misl period in detail, some elements of their story has differing circumstances. In the case of some, several events are dateless or dated varyingly while names of some key historical figures spelt differently. One historian provides contradictory narrative of the same event. Some historians omitted the story of individual misls per se. Instead, they describe misl activities vis-à-vis Afghan invaders.

---

[13] The Sikhs by Patwant Singh 1999 (John Murray)
[14] History of the Sikhs by J.D. Cunningham 1985 (S. Chand & Company Ltd)

For example, Khushwant Singh misses out the misl period and provides no separate mention of individual misls or their raison d'etre or strengths and weaknesses, with the sole exception of Sukerchakia misl.[15] Rather the Afghan invader Ahmad Shah Abdali strides across his narrative, a star figure of his two lengthy chapters, with supporting roles featuring Sikh misldars, and, even in that regard, it is the incidental interactions between the two archenemies that are interspersed throughout the telling of the Afghan invasions.

Even though Dr. Gopal Singh devotes an entire 27-page chapter to the misl period, he, too, ignores discussion of individual misls per se.[16] His attempt to weave together different strands of misl activity is a patchwork quilt without design, a mere account of fleeting misl episodes. Thus, his narrative while informative it is fractured and difficult to comprehend.

One historian who spared no detail in providing an exhaustive perspective of misl history, misl by misl, and their formation into a commonwealth is Syed Muhammad Latif.[17] Although he provides analyses of individual misls at macro level, his narrative in each

---

[15] A History of the Sikhs by Khushwant Singh 1963 – Vol. 1 (Princeton University Press)
[16] A History of Sikh People by Dr. Gopal Singh 1979 - World Sikh University Press
[17] History of the Punjab – From the Remotest Antiquity to the Present Time by Syed Muhammad Latif 1891 – Progressive Books

case is a collection of stories that do not necessarily cohere with one another. There is no common thread revealing subtle interplay between the antagonists; the chronology of unfolding of some key events is unclear; and, to get a proper perspective of some of the inter-connected events requires navigating from one chapter to another.

In his admirable biography of Jassa Singh Ahluwalia, Ganda Singh covers the misl period but largely through the prism of the life and times of the Ahluwalia chieftain and his confrontation with the Mogul and Afghan foes.[18] Sohan Singh Seetal devotes one chapter to each misl in his seventeen-chapter book but with no chapter on the pre-eminent Sukerchakia misl, which eventually formed the Sikh kingdom.[19]

History is a catalogue of noteworthy events, a kaleidoscope of victors, and the vanquished. Credibility of an event depends on reliability of the information. A first-hand source, usually an eyewitness, deserves greater relevance and weight. Next is hearsay information, which is a happening not witnessed by the writer but rather learned about it from someone else and is verifiable. Least valuable is unsubstantiated information.

---

[18] Sardar Jassa Singh Ahluwalia by Ganda Singh 1990 – Punjab University Patiala
[19] The Sikh Misls and the Panjab by Sohan Singh Seetal 1981 – Majha Printing Press

Western historians and writers believe that only a document written first-hand to describe an event memorializes a fact. Since the Normans carried out an extensive survey of who owned what to determine what taxes need to be levied (known as Domesday Book) the English have embraced the written tradition to record important socio-political and economic history. They do not put much stock in second-hand knowledge unless supported by another plausible source.

Eyewitness observations of same event may vary as every spectator views it from a different perspective because of individual-specific bias. Their recall of the sequence of events or chronology may also vary. Some may meticulously describe the order in which a series of events happened while others may omit mention of an aspect either because it slipped their mind or was not worthy of mention.

Inevitable, also, is that as the memory is passed down the hearer may embellish the incident by adding or subtracting something to beautify the event.[20] The

---

[20] According to Purnima Dhavan the anecdote involving estrangement of Jassa Singh Ramgarhia from the Khalsa community following his role in female infanticide "must be treated with caution, since it appears in a much later source, Giani Gian Singh's *Tawarikh Guru Khal;sa: Bhag Duja*. She writes: Giani Gian Singh himself notes uncertainty regarding the authenticity of the story, but offers it as explanation for Jassa Singh's service with Adina Beg Khan, reflecting a latter-day discomfort with the notion of a Sikh officer in Mughal service - When Sparrows Became Hawks: The Making of the Sikh Warrior

probability of an error between two memories is highly possible but should not be a reason to dismiss them in entirety. In some cases, the delay in reporting an event after a lapse of time may reduce the value of the account itself. What is imperative is to know that a sequence of events did occur.

All cultures and peoples of the world transmit their memories to their descendents in oral lore. Written technology has now preserved these oral memories for all times. What deserves due contemplation is the writer's bias expressed in terms of additions or omissions. For example, the Gospels of Matthew and John, who were part of the twelve Disciples of Christ, differ significantly from one another in theme, content, time duration, order of events. John's account of the life of Christ is set entirely in Judea whereas Matthew's record is set principally in Galilee. Provided these differently construed narratives do not belie the ethos of the life and times of Christ, the impact of the differences may be insignificant.

History, literature, memories, folklore passed through the generations by word of mouth in ancient India, because society of that era was unfamiliar with the tools of writing. Incorporating of that orally rendered Indian knowledge into a written account had its unintended consequences. For instance, wider the time-elapse between the event and its chronicling the greater the likelihood of increased embellishing and

---

Tradition 1699-1799 by Purnima Dhavan - Oxford University Press, 2011 – page 82 and its endnote

discrepancy in the narrative. Eyewitness accounts may differ between those who observed the event or entail a slightly different spectator version of the same sequence of a happening or statements. Again, the parallelism in the account of two or more people will likely be askew. Lack of conformity does not suggest that the event did not take place but rather that personal remembrances are frail. Hence, imperfections and gaps in the narrative should receive less emphasis and the core ingredient or underpinning memory greater emphasis.

Indian historians respect the oral tradition. However, western-trained historians tend to make light of historical accounts derived from oral sources viewing such accounts of not meeting the threshold of meticulousness; some accounts criticized for being too hagiographic.[21]

Idealizing biographies, coloured embellishments, inconsistencies, contradictions between historians, gaps in narratives and distrust of oral traditions prejudice our understanding of the ascendancy of Sikh power in Punjab in the 18th century.

---

[21] Purnima Dhavan believes that our understanding of the ideas understood and implemented by Sikhs remain on shaky grounds, shaped largely by a narrative of the Khalsa's origins and history pulled together from later hagiographic sources. Scholars have long noted the discrepancies and problems with the sources of this narrative of the Khalsa's origins - When Sparrows Became Hawks: The Making of the Sikh Warrior Tradition - page 3-4

Purnima Dhavan, Assistant Professor, University of Washington has waded into this murky period, providing a fresh and differing perspectives of key events lacking clarity. She examines the crucial period between the death of Guru Gobind Singh and the creation of the Sikh empire; less enthralled by how the misls came into being and more occupied with the internecine warfare between fragmented misl leaders. Her insight into the kaleidoscopic nature of "competing ideologies, political agendas, and cultural preferences (that) frequently emerged as Sikh rulers, authors, and peasant soldiers attempted to come to terms with how Khalsa identity would be formalized and who in the community would have influence over directing its affairs" is penetrating indeed.[22]

The recounting of the events and memories underscoring the militarization of Punjab peasantry and assertion of Sikh hegemony over Punjab by aforementioned historians and writers may sometimes be at odds; nonetheless, it does not detract from constructing a telling chronological narrative.

To understand the nuances of the times we need first to understand the idea of Punjab.

---

[22] A paper titled "Investing in Sikh Studies: Rewards and Challenges for a New Generation of Scholars" presented at "Opportunities and Challenges for Sikh Academics," (2010).

2 - PUNJAB: a hallowed land, an Eden lost

Punjab is sacred ground to Sikhs because within it lays Harminder Sahib (Golden Temple), the spiritual centre of the Sikhs; Akal Takht, the centre of temporal authority; Anandpur Sahib, the birthplace of the Khalsa. Other key Gurdwaras are located in West Punjab, Pakistan: including but not limited to, Nankana Sahib, birthplace of the first Guru, Nanak Dev; and, Gurdwara Punj Sahib, located 35 kilometers north-west of Islamabad. Equally revered is Gurdwara Sis Gunj in Old Delhi, memorializing the spot of beheading of the ninth Guru Teg Bahadur. All of the Sikh Gurus except one were born in undivided Punjab.

Punjab lies wedged between Hindu Kush Mountains and the subcontinent of India. The high mountain passes that straddle these two worlds (Khyber Pass, Chitral Pass, Dorah Pass and Shandur Pass) lured many invaders, among them Aryans of Central Steppe, Greeks led by Alexander the Great, Scythians, White Huns, Persians, Afghans and the descendants of Genghis Khan. Of this mountain passes Khyber Pass stood squarely in the path of the nomad settler (e.g. Aryan, Scythian); traders plying the Silk Road; conquerors (e.g. Alexander, the Turk Mahmud of Ghazni, the Afghan Lodi, the Moguls and the British); and, the pillagers (e.g. Ahmad Shah Abdali).

From antiquity until Babur's invasion of India Punjab as such had no identity; its geo-political boundaries not yet delineated. "Until the 15th century Punjab had only two important cities, Lahore, which was the seat of most governments, and Multan in the South, which had a busy market dealing with commerce coming up the rivers from Sindh and caravans from Baluchistan and Persia".[23]

From Middle Ages the northern region of the Indian sub-continent was known by the name "Hindustan", a word derived from the two Persian words 'Hindu', itself a variant of Sindhu, the Sanskrit name by which Indus River was known, and the suffix 'stan', a variant of Persian word 'sthana', meaning land. Thus, all Turkic-Afghan invaders, from Mahmud of Ghazni to Babur, entered the subcontinent via the Khyber Pass to invade the land they called Hindustan.

The Mogul rulers likely coined the word Punjab influenced by the topography of the land through which five rivers course their way to merge with the great Indus River. The word is derived from the Persian which was the language of the Mogul darbar (court) by the combination of two Persian words "Punj" denoting five and "Ab" meaning water to describe the land of five rivers (Jhelum, Chenab, Ravi, Beas and Sutlej).

---

[23] A History of the Sikhs by Khushwant Singh – Vol. 1 p.8

Described by its topography, Punjab features "Doabs or intra-fluvial tracts, which form the natural divisions of the country (and) names which were given them in the days of Mogul ascendancy".[24] Doabs literally means land of two rivers. "Thus the tract between Bias and Ravi is called Bari Doab, that between the Ravi and Chenab the Rechna Doab, that between the Chenab and Jhelum the Chaj Doab", and the land between Beas and Sutlej Bist Doab.[25]

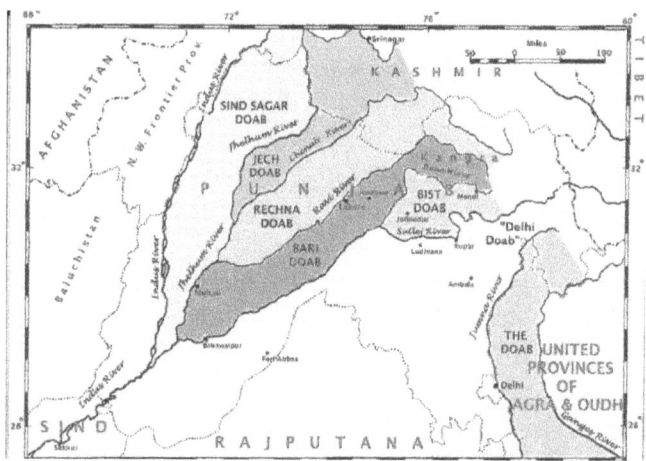

Pictorially speaking, Punjab looks like a V-shaped cone, tilted on its side, with Panjnad River forming the tip of the cone - a place where five rivers of Punjab flow together to become Panjnad River before

---

[24] History of the Punjab by Syed Muhammad Latif published 1891 – p.11
[25] *ibid* – p.11

joining the Indus at Mithankot (Pakistan). The northern sloping side of the wide opening at the top represents Jhelum River and the southern sloping side represents Sutlej and the other three rivers in betwixt the two. The conical-shaped Punjab represents the topography of Punjab, a terrain and surface that is eternal.

There are no known cartographical maps of Punjab of antiquity. Political boundaries had not come into being. There was no nation state and no land divided on linguistic or ethnical lines. The gateway to the subcontinent was like a turnstile through which invaders and marauders came and went. Because of continual ebb and flow of conquerors, no one left a lasting legacy.

In fact, the land was a patchwork quilts of diverse communities stitched together through subjugation. Serial conquests and expansion or contraction reshaped these fluid patches. Akbar was the first ruler to introduce some semblance of governable administration, primarily after he had enlarged his domain through conquest.

In the earlier part of their rule, the Moguls had no solid footprint in Punjab or Cis-Sutlej region. The suzerainty of Humayun, who succeeded Babar, was limited to Kabul, parts of Punjab and Delhi and Agra and their environs. When Humayun passed away his son Akbar was a minor and this was the cue to the Afghans led by the brilliant Hindu General Hemu

Chandra Bhargav to wrest away Delhi and Agra from the Moguls.

In October 1556, Hemu set himself as Maharaja in the fort of Delhi, taking up the title of Vikramaditya. He thus became "the only Hindu to occupy the throne of Delhi during the medieval period of our history".[26] However, Hemu's victory was short-lived. One month later (November 1556), Akbar, guided by his guardian Bairam Khan, defeated Hemu in the second battle of Panipat and then dispensed with the Afghan pretenders to the "sovereignty of Hindustan".

Akbar was the most politically perceptive ruler of medieval India. In 1602 he established a hierarchical system of government by dividing his empire "into well-defined provinces (that) numbered fifteen (that included) Lahore, Multan and Malwa".[27] This was the beginning of forming of Punjab as a political entity.

Malwa region was home to several tribal groups, among them Gandharas, Kambojas, Sauviras, Madras, Trigartas, and Rajputs. Punjabi farmers marginalized in Punjab proper, prompted by agrarian impulse, had drifted across the Sutlej into Malwa. The Punjabi presence in Malwa was noticeable.

At its height, Maharaja Ranjit Singh's empire extended in the east up to Sutlej River. The Mogul ruler manipulated by the puppeteer British controlled the

---

[26] The Mogul Empire by Ashirbadilal Srivastava – p. 132-135
[27] Ibid. – p.185

Cis-Sutlej, which included Malwa: "the British thus became the only real power on the Punjab's eastern frontier, with nothing but the conglomeration of Malwa chiefs between them and Lahore Durbar".[28]

The political map of Punjab has undergone radical changes. At its zenith, Maharaja Ranjit Singh's empire had stretched a little to the west of the Indus River incorporating Peshawar in the north-west, Dera Ismail Khan in mid-west and Dera Ghazi Khan in south-west, and bounded in the east by Sutlej River.

Punjab greatly expanded under British rule. Although the line demarcating its western boundary was more or less same as that of Maharaja Ranjit Singh, it had in the east extended to the Jamna River and in southeast almost to the doorsteps of Delhi. It encompassed the principalities of Patiala, Kapurthala, Faridkot, Nabha, and Jind.

In 1947, the pact of Indian Independence stipulated the partition of Punjab into two regions: western region covering two-thirds area going to Pakistan (West Punjab) and eastern region amounting to one-third to India (East Punjab). These two nations share, in part, two rivers: Ravi and Sutlej. The western boundary of East Punjab is bounded in the north partly by Ravi River that meanders around district Gurdaspur and veers away into Pakistan some 10 Km north of Atari; and, in the south-west the Sutlej river

---

[28] A History of the Sikhs by Khushwant Singh – Vol. 1 p.212

flowing through East Punjab pivots away into Pakistan near Fazilka.

It is an irony that the areas that Sikh misls (confederacy) shed their blood to wrest control of from the Afghans, Marathas and the Moguls - including but not limited to Gujranwala, Sialkot Gujrat, Sargodha, Kasur, Pakpattan, Multan and Bahawalpur – are lost forever by being made an integral part of Pakistan.

Since independence, Punjab has thrice undergone further splits. First, in 1948 thirty princely states of northern Punjab removed and merged into Himachal Pradesh. Second, in 1966 several districts of Punjab (e.g. Hissar, Gurgaon, Rohtak, and Karnal) carved out to create the state of Haryana. Third, in 1971, some other hilly areas of Punjab (e.g. Simla, Kangra, Kulu, and areas from Hoshiarpur, Gurdaspur, and Ambala) allotted to Himachal Pradesh that further enlarged that province at the expense of Punjab.

Punjab survives in the topography of the continent and in the historical context but ceases to exist in the political context. Eviscerated by politics Punjab's new political geometry is vastly different from days of fore. The land is a victim of geopolitics. Today's reality is that only four rivers (Jhelum, Chenab, Ravi and Sutlej) flow through West Punjab province of Pakistan and, if described by topography, it is Char-ab (land of four rivers); and, since only three rivers stream through East Punjab State of India (Ravi, Beas and Sutlej) it is Teen-ab (land of three rivers).

3 - Evolving of a Warrior-Saint Culture

Mogul Emperor Akbar's death by dysentery in the last week of October 1605 set in motion a train of disasters. First among the victims was Akbar's policy on religious tolerance that had irked the Muslim orthodoxy. It also precipitated a political crisis, as Salim, the only surviving son of Akbar, who on accession in November 1605 assumed the title of Jahangir, was to face rebellion of his eldest son Khusrav.

The rebellion was short lived and all those who supported and succored Khusrav were to face Jahangir's wrath. Among the accused was Guru Arjun Dev.[29] It so happened that during a stopover at Taran Taran, en route to Lahore, Guru Arjun warmly received Khusrav. When Jahangir got wind of that meeting, he levied a fine on the Guru. The Guru refuted the charge of treason and refused to pay the fine, whereupon Jahangir had the Guru arrested and put to death by torture in the summer of 1606.

---

[29] During his extensive traveling around central Punjab "Arjun brought into his fold thousands of Jats of the Majha country, the sturdiest peasants of the Punjab" - A History of the Sikhs by Khushwant Singh – Vol. 1 page 57

The martyred death of Guru Arjun Dev would represent a paradigm shift in Sikh psyche.[30] His eleven-year-old orphaned son, Hargobind, assumed the guruship and in keeping with his father's injunction sat "fully armed on his throne and maintain an army". He girded two swords round his waist: one signifying piri (derived from Persian word 'pir' meaning a holy man) and, therefore signifying spiritual power and the other epitomizing miri (of Persian origin, denoting governance, and civil authority) and, accordingly, representing temporal power.[31]

While Khushwant Singh and Dr. Gopal Singh are in consonant with Surjit Singh Gandhi on the point of Hargobind girded with the two swords at his investiture, Patwant Singh and Purnima Dhavan hold entirely different versions.

---

[30] "The Sikh tradition attributes the punishment to Jahangir's religious bigotry and alleges that it was accompanied by barbarous torture. These allegations are without foundation. But the Guru's death estranged his followers from the Mughuls and led to their rebellion in the time of Aurengzeb" - The Mogul Empire by Ashirbadilal Srivastava – p. 259

[31] At his investiture, Baba Buddha brought Hargobind, a *seli* (a woolen cord worn as a necklace or twisted around the head by former Gurus and a turban as *'appurtenances'* of his calling. Guru Hargobind then addressed Baba Buddha "My *seli* will be my sword belt and I shall wear the turban with a royal aigrette". He wore two swords – one symbolizing *piri*, spiritual power, and the other signifying *miri*, the temporal power. There *deg* (kettle) or meals for friends and *teg* (sword) or punishment for foes would always be ready – History of Sikh Gurus Retold: 1606-1708 CE by Surjit Singh Gandhi – p.474-475

Purnima Dhavan believes that following Hargobind's release from Gwalior prison, where the Guru was interned by Emperor Jahangir for not paying the fine that was imposed on his father, that "the sixth Guru formulated the policy of miri-piri, which described the sovereignty of the Guru over both the spiritual (piri) and worldly (miri) affairs of the Panth (Sikh collectivity) ".[32]

According to Patwant Singh, following his investiture, the Guru started establishing "intensive training camps for swordsmanship, archery, and physical endurance" which the Guru felt "was necessary if the religion was to be saved from those wanting to destroy it". It was "out of this awareness emerged Hargobind's concept of meeri and peeri".[33]

At the time Harminder Sahib (temple of God, derived from the Sanskrit word 'Hari' meaning God), completed in 1601 by Guru Arjun Dev, symbolizing piri, was the spiritual centre of the Sikhs. In 1606, Guru Hargobind in furtherance of his idea of miri built the Akal Takht (the eternal throne). Akal Takht, seat of temporal power, stands facing Harminder Sahib.

Guru Hargobind held court at the Akal Takht, where he heard the pleas of his followers, adjudicated

---

[32] When Sparrows Became Hawks: The Making of the Sikh Warrior Tradition 1699-1799 - Oxford University Press, 2011 – page 31
[33] Patwant Singh "the Sikhs" at page 40

disputes, issued Hukamnamas (decrees), and met dignitaries. In the evening, Akal Takht echoed with ballads and songs in praise of courage, gallantry, and indomitable spirit. The Guru popularized the singing of the 'var' (ode) to the rhythmic beat of the dhad, a small hourglass-shaped drum. The melodious rendition of traditional ballads extolling the heroic deeds of warriors and heroes were not just uplifting, encouraging, and inspirational they helped boost the spirits of the congregants.

Guru Hargobind wanted to imbue his followers with military zeal. He introduced a regimen of weaponry and combats training, tactics of guerilla warfare and horsemanship. To sharpen the skills of his retinue he arranged hunting expeditions. Followers were encouraged to donate arms and horses.[34]

---

[34] The Guru intended Sikhs in general and Sikh soldiers in particular to imbibe martial spirit and acquire physical fitness. He made daily exercise an important part of the daily routine of the Sikhs. He marked a piece if land just facing Akal Takht to serve as *akhara* (wrestling ground), where wrestling and other physical exercises were done. For the recruits of the army, Guru introduced rigorous training in different arts of war-archery, horsemanship, swordsmanship, and throwing of lances arranged under the direct supervision of the Guru's commanders.... The Guru also trained his soldiers in war-crafts e.g. selection of ground for positioning forces, formation of forces according to enemy positions, determining frontage, patrolling, intelligence, organizing sorties and camouflage, communication, psychological warfare et al - History of Sikh Gurus Retold: 1606-1708 CE by Surjit Singh Gandhi – p.484-486

In time, Guru Hargobind had built up a powerful militia. At times his militia allied with Mogul forces on imperial expeditions and on some other times prompted by zeitgeist, they accosted local Mogul commanders. Thus, "long before the creation of the Khalsa, we have the beginnings of an armed group within the Panth and growing opposition to imperial authority".[35]

Henceforth, the exigency of protecting the faith became the paradigm. "The right to defend the faith by force of arms" according to Khushwant Singh, "proved to be extremely popular", which was a lure for the "assertive and virile race" of Punjabis, legions of whom embraced the Guru.[36]

The growing militarization of the Sikhs did not escape the notice of the Mogul functionaries who made mention of it in their dispatches to the Emperor. On the pretext that the Guru had not discharged the fine outstanding against his father, Guru Arjun, Jehangir issued a warrant for the arrest of Guru Hargobind and ordered demobilizing of his militia. The Guru

---

[35] When Sparrows Became Hawks: The Making of the Sikh Warrior Tradition 1699-1799 - Oxford University Press, 2011 – page 30

[36] "The number of Sikhs had been steadily increasing with each Guru. The change of emphasis from a peaceful propagation of the faith to the forthright declaration of the right to defend that faith by force of arms proved to be extremely popular…….Hargobind infused in them (Punjabis) the confidence that they could challenge the might of the Mogul Emperor" - A History of the Sikhs by Khushwant Singh – Vol. 1 p.66

apprehended and jailed for a year or so. On his release, the Guru resumed his temporal pursuits discreetly and in time assembled a sizeable fighting force.[37]

In 1628, Shah Jahan was crowned emperor. The same year Guru Hargobind and Shah Jahan came to lock horns in a hunting episode. The scene of encounter has variegated versions[38]. Guru's guards rallied and beat back the Mogul posse, killing the Chief Constable Mukhlis Khan. Fearful of the fallout from the slaying of Mukhlis Khan and hoping to avoid putting Harminder Sahib in harm's way Hargobind left Amritsar for Kartarpur, a town located 16 Km north-west of Jullundur.

---

[37] In his work *Dabistan-e-Mazahib*, Mogul historian Mohsin Fani writes: "the Guru had 800 horses in his stables, 300 troops on horseback and 60 men with forearms were in his service".

[38] Patwant Singh describes the scene in following words: "Shah Jahan and the Guru had been hunting in the vicinity of Amritsar and a dispute between their followers – each of whom claimed the rare white hawk – led to an encounter. An annoyed emperor dispatched a detachment of troops under Mukhlis Khan to arrest the Guru" (The Sikhs by Patwant Singh – p.41). It is a mystery why the emperor did not chose to settle the incident then and there.

Khushwant Singh's version is that "In 1628 when Shah Jahan happened to be hunting in the neighborhood of Amritsar, his men clashed with the retainers of the Guru. A bailiff and a posse of constabulary were sent to arrest the Guru" (A History of the Sikhs by Khushwant Singh – Vol. 1 p.65). This account stands to reason in that the altercation involved followers of the Guru. Guru was not a participant in the hunting expedition, which explains why a posse was sent to the residence of the Guru.

Over the following five years, Guru Hargobind clashed with the Moguls on two occasions (at Lahira in 1631 and Kartarpur in 1634) and on both times the Mogul assailants were defeated. The second encounter was much more devastating for the Moguls as it resulted in the slaying of their commander Painde Khan. Exigency created by the killing persuaded the Guru to repair to Kiratpur.

Kiratpur lies on the bank of the Sutlej River, in the foothills of Shivalik hills, about10 Km southeast of present day Anandpur Sahib. Here the Guru had built a safe haven that he named Kiratpur (abode of praise), a place where he was to spend remainder of his life (1634-1644).[39]

Before he passed away in March 1644, Guru Hargobind anointed his 14-year old grandson Har Rai to take over the guruship. Born and raised in Kiratpur, Har Rai was the younger of the two sons of

---

[39] A History of the Sikhs by Khushwant Singh – Vol. 1 p.66
The name Shivalik (also spelled Siwalik) means "belonging to Shiva". Geologically speaking, Shivalik hills or range, also called Outer Himalayas, form a chain that extends 1,600 Km from Sikkim across north western India into Pakistan
According to W.H. McLeod, when the Guru relocated to Shivalik in 1634, "from this time onwards Guru Hargobind and all four of his successors spent most of their time in Shivalik Hills. It was in these hills that the tenth Guru was brought up, for most of his period as Guru he was exclusively occupied in Shivalik affairs. Only towards the end did Mogul force from Sirhind enter what was essentially a Shivalik Hills war" (Sikhs and Sikhism – essay on The Evolution of the Sikh Community p.13).

Gurditta, himself the only son of Guru Hargobind. Gurditta passed way in 1638 and survived by two sons: Dhirmal and Har Rai. Dhirmal, the older brother, had betrayed his grandfather; wherefore Har Rai became the chosen successor.

Har Rai got into conflict with Aurengzeb during the Mogul war of succession to the throne of his father, Emperor Shah Jahan.[40] The showing of empathy by Guru Har Rai with Dara Shikoh, the eldest son and heir-apparent, had so piqued Aurengzeb that on occupying the throne he ordered the Guru to be brought to his court at Delhi. The Guru sent his elder son, Ram Rai, in his stead.

Aurengzeb required of Ram Rai to explain a certain scriptural quotation from the Granth Sahib (sacred scriptures) that contained a word that a Muslim would find offensive. Ram Rai interchanged the offensive word with a benign one. The knowledge of the incident of alteration of the context of the hymn of Guru Nanak upset Guru Har Rai, prompting him to ostracize his son and proclaim his youngest son Hari Krishen as his successor.

---

[40] Shah Jahan fell sick in September 1657 and rumour spread that he was dead. Believing he was at death's doorstep Shah Jahan appointed his eldest son Dara Shikoh regent. The other three sons, governors of provinces with considerable resources and following, took measures to wrest the crown. Aurengzeb finally prevailed. He had his father, the Emperor, confined to Shah Burj of the Agra fort for eight years until his death in January 1666 - The Mogul Empire by Ashirbadilal Srivastava – p. 321-322.

On the passing of Har Rai, in 1661, Aurengzeb "wanted to play a decisive role in the affairs of the Sikhs" and decided to interpose himself as an arbitrator in the matter of succession to the guruship. The plan came to naught when the 8-year old Guru Hari Krishen died of smallpox. Before he died he chose as his successor "an older man living in the village of Bakala" with the intention of bypassing pretenders Dhirmal or Ram Rai.[41]

The "old man of Bakala" was Tegh Bahadur, the youngest of five sons of sixth Guru Hargobind. At age 45, he assumed the guruship. His ascension to guruship faced a roiling internecine strife (e.g., Dhirmal plotted his murder). He was made unwelcome to Harminder Sahib by the masands (vicars in charge of congregation and offerings) and to Kiratpur by contentious relatives.

On a grassy knoll, not far from Kiratpur, Guru Tegh Bahadur built his own abode that he named Anandpur (haven of bliss), but bliss was to elude him as he was continually pestered by his relatives.[42] He

---

[41] A History of the Sikhs by Khushwant Singh – Vol. 1 p.70
[42] ibid – p.71
Surjit Singh Gandhi describes the founding of *Anandpur* in following words, "The Guru was received with utmost respect by Rani Champa who did all she could to make the Guru's three days stay as comfortable as possible. During his stay, the Guru expressed that he would like to build a new settlement near Kiratpur and offered to buy a suitable piece of land for that purpose" which he eventually obtained by paying 500 rupees. "The foundation of the new settlement was laid by Baba Gurditta, the son of Baba Budha on 19 June 1665. This new

left his haven in August 1665 and traveled eastwards through several places teaching the gospel. When he arrived in the old city of Patna (known as Pataliputra in ancient times) his wife was pregnant. He arranged for her and his mother (Mata Nanaki) to stay behind in Patna while he continued his journey to other places in the east. He was in Dacca (now the capital of Bangladesh) when he received the news of birth of his son who was named Gobind Rai. For another three years, he continued the work of his ministry in Assam, returning briefly to Patna before heading homewards to Punjab.

The Punjab that Guru Tegh Bahadur returned to early in 1672 was in turmoil.[43] Everywhere he went he heard tales of woe. He became a vociferous opponent of the unjust taxes and championed the rights of the

---

settlement was named Chak Nanaki, after the revered name of Guru's mother. The humble beginnings served as nucleus for the beautiful town of *Anandpur* which subsequently grew around it" (History of Sikh Gurus Retold: 1606-1708 C.E - p.628)
The Guru had gone to Bilaspur to mourn the death of Raja Dip Chand; Rani Champa was the dowager Rani.
[43] In 1679 Aurengzeb promulgated an order re-imposing *jiziya* (head or poll tax) on Hindus…..many Hindus who could not pay the *jiziya* became Muhammadans….he also re-imposed the pilgrim's tax… (reinstated) customs duties in the case of Hindus….in 1671 he prohibited Hindu religious fairs and festivals and in the same year all Hindus, except Rajputs, were forbidden to ride in palanquins, on elephants and good horses and forbidden to carry arms. Thus Aurengzeb put every kind of pressure on the Hindus in order to induce their conversion to Islam….ordered the Sikh temples to be destroyed and *masands* to be expelled from the cities - The Mogul Empire by Ashirbadilal Srivastava – p. 334-337

poor. Hindus flocked to listen to his sermons and he heard complaints of coercion to embrace Islam. The case of Hindus of Kashmir, however, compelled immediate attention.

On May 25 1675, a delegation of Kashmiri pandits led by Kirpa Ram made their way to Anandpur to make the Guru aware of how diligently Iftikhar Khan, governor of Kashmir, was enforcing Aurengzeb's firman (edict) to Islamize Kashmir. They beseeched Guru Tegh Bahadur to save the Hindu religion.

Guru Tegh Bahadur proclaimed "the inalienable right of a people to practice their own faith could not be denied to them by bigoted rulers" and threw "down the gauntlet" declaring that "if the emperor could make him convert to Islam, the pandits too would accept conversion". Aurangzeb was "enraged by reports of Guru Tegh Bahadur's sympathetic response to the Kashmiris, ordered him to be brought to Delhi".[44]

---

[44] The Sikhs by Patwant Singh – p.47
Surjit Singh Gandhi recounts the meeting in following words:
"There is a strong tradition that Guru Tegh Bahadur, on hearing the heart rending tale of Kashmiri pandits, was deeply absorbed in pondering over the problem. Suddenly the young Gobind Rai entered the Darbar and was astonished at the complete silence reigning everywhere. After a brief pause, he quietly enquired from his father as to the cause of this silence. The Guru explained to the boy the agony of the pandits and significantly remarked that the only way was that some great person should make supreme sacrifice. The boy asked his father whether there was anybody more worthy of this sacrifice than himself. The hint was very clear. The Guru appreciated the bold and courageous

On July 12th 1675 the Guru and his companions were arrested by the Kotwal (Chief Constable) of Ropar and sent to Sirhind where they were placed in the custody of the faujdar (military administrator) Dilawar Khan, and transported to Delhi in an iron cage about four months later. In November, a disconsolate Guru witnessed the brutal death of each of his three companions. The qazi (Judge) offered to reprieve the Guru if he would embrace Islam. Guru refused to yield whereupon he was tortured and beheaded. This was to be a watershed in Sikh history, captured poetically and vividly by Guru Gobind in Bachitra Natak.

Guruship devolved upon nine-year-old orphaned son, Gobind Rai. In 1685 Guru and his entourage left Anandpur and relocated to Paonta, a place on the banks of Jamna River in the foothills of Himalaya, about 90 Km north-east of Rishikesh, now part of present day Himachal Pradesh. There is disagreement

---

reply of his son and forthwith decided to offer himself of the sacrifice. He told the Brahmins to go home and tell the authorities that they would have no objection to changing their religion if Guru Tegh Bahadur was first prevailed upon to embrace Islam" - (History of Sikh Gurus Retold: 1606-1708 C.E - p.659-660).
The depiction of the aforementioned incident is corroborated by Harbans Singh in his book Guru Gobind Singh at page 16 "The Kashmiri Pandits were the most literate section of the Hindu population which led the rulers to believe that, if they were brought into the fold of Islam, the task of converting the rest of the people would become easier" – Guru Gobind Singh by Harbans Singh, p. 17

among historians as to what prompted Guru Gobind to take up abode in Paonta.

Khushwant Singh, for example, explains that the leaders of the community were fearful of the Mogul taking young Guru as a hostage and removing him to Delhi. Therefore, "To avoid any chances, the young Guru and his entourage were shifted from Anandpur further into the mountains at Paonta".[45]

Gopal Singh presents an altogether contrasting story. He believes it is "ridiculous in the extreme" to assert that the Guru was "removed to Paonta" because of fear of being seized "as a hostage". He suggests that the Raja of Nahan invited the Guru "as he was inimical to Raja Fateh Shah of Srinagar and wanted Guru's assistance, should he be attacked". That caused the Guru to proceed to Nahan accompanied by "his family and five hundred armed men mostly Udasis".[46]

Harbans Singh has a different story to tell. According to him, the Guru was invited by Raja Medini Prakash, ruler of Sirmur, to spend some time with him at Nahan, a town about 60 Km north-east of Ambala, to enjoy its cool air and hunting game. The Guru set forth "accompanied by his relatives and a body of trained Sikhs". One day while hunting the Guru chanced upon a place by the banks of Jamna River

---

[45] A History of the Sikhs by Khushwant Singh – Vol. 1 p.76
   Paonta means a foot stool or resting place
[46] A History of the Sikh People by Dr. Gopal Singh – p.266

with which he was so enraptured that he decided to make it his domicile.[47]

Guru Gobind had no territory to rule per se. Both of his two residences were located in the Shivalik hills: Anandpur fell in the domain of Raja Bhim Chand of Bilaspur while Paonta was part of the principality of Raja Medini Prakash of Sirmur. He devoted a good deal of time in religious schooling, martial and weapons training of his followers. He promoted recreational activities including hunting. Over time, he had a sizeable fighting force. All these goings-on did not escape the notice of the Shivalik hill chieftains and aroused their suspicions of Guru's agenda.

Among the hill chiefs, Raja Bhim Chand of Bilaspur and Raja Fateh Shah of Srinagar in particular, harboured a feeling of anger and ill will towards the Guru. They felt threatened by Guru Gobind's caste-blind attitude and egalitarian teachings, which may put at risk their privileged way of life. They were also fearful of the large armed force commanded by the Guru.

Following the nuptials of Raja Bhim Chand's son to the daughter of Fateh Shah, the two chiefs conspired to launch an attack on the Guru at Paonta. In September 1688, the hill chiefs marched towards Paonta and met by Guru Gobind's forces at

---

[47] Guru Gobind Singh by Harbans Singh – p.28-29
Guru reached the vicinity of Nahan on April 14, 1685. He was nineteen years old.

Bhangani, a place six miles from Paonta. Five hundred of Pathan soldiers deserted the Guru and joined the hill Rajas, and concurrently most of the Udasi contingent took to flight.[48] However, the dire situation ameliorated as Pir Buddhu Shah of Sadhaura came to Guru's rescue accompanied by his four sons. The battle of Bhangani raged on fiercely and it was the valour and tenacity of Guru's forces that routed the army of the hill Rajas.[49]

The date of the Battle of Bhangani is in dispute. Khushwant Singh has a date in 1686.[50] Harbans Singh, on the other hand, is precise in saying it took place on September 18 1688.[51] In his footnote at page 270, Gopal Singh says that Mahan Kosh corroborates the date in late April 1689 but then immediately discounts it in favour of September 1688 on the authority of an article by Dr. Kirpal Singh published in the January 1967 issue of The Sikh Review.

Guru Gobind departed Paonta in 1689 to return to Ananadpur, never to set foot in Paonta again. He was dismayed to find a flock of followers at Anandpur

---

[48] The Pathan contingent, demobilized from the Mogul army, were commended to the Guru's favour by Pir Buddhu Shah - Guru Gobind Singh by Harbans Singh – p.35

[49] The battle vividly narrated in *Bachitra Natak*. The conclusion of the battle described in these words: "I took up my bow and began to discharge arrows. Upon this my adversaries began to flee. I took aim and discharged an arrow. The young chief Hari Chand was killed. The hill men fled in consternation. The victory was mine, through Thy favour, Akal".

[50] A History of the Sikhs by Khushwant Singh – Vol. 1 p.78

[51] Guru Gobind Singh by Harbans Singh – p.37

much reduced. As word of Guru's return to Anandpur spread, people came in droves from all over the country to pay their respect. Guru immersed himself in reconstituting his warriors and building fortresses.

Noting that Aurengzeb was preoccupied in the recovery of his Deccan territories (Bijapur and Golkunda) and subduing the Marathas, the hill chiefs stopped paying tribute to the Mogul government. Mian Khan, Governor of Jammu, tasked his commander Alif Khan to enforce performance on the defaulters.

While most of the hill chiefs yielded to the Mogul authority, Bhim Chand, Raja of Bilaspur, remained defiant. He had earlier mended fences with Guru Gobind and appealed to the Guru for help. On March 20 1691, the combined forces of the Raja and the Guru intercepted the Mogul forces led by Alif Khan, at Nadaun, on the eastern bank of Beas River, some 40 Km south of Kangra. The Guru in his words describes the rout of the Mogul forces: "the Almighty God hastened the end of the fight and the opposing host was driven away into the river without having the chance to care for his camp".[52]

Here again, there is a lack of consensus to the date of the Battle of Nadaun. Khushwant Singh believes that

---

[52] Guru Gobind Singh by Harbans Singh – p.39

the battle fought in 1687.[53] Gopal Singh is vague and unclear by maintaining it was "probably late in 1690".[54] Harbans Singh is explicit that the battle took place on March 20, 1691.

On a date not settled, but one soon after the Battle of Nadaun, Guru Gobind secluded himself at Naina Devi, a place 12 Km north-east of Anandpur, perched on a hilltop at an elevation of 1,200 meters. In the quiet silence of the lofty peak, he composed Bachitra Natak (meaning wondrous play or drama) and reflected deeply "over the disunity and decadence that had come into the movement launched by Nanak (and) wrangling over the succession to the guruship and the masands".[55]

Guru Gobind emerged from seclusion with a conceived mental image of whither to steer his faith.

---

[53] A History of the Sikhs by Khushwant Singh – Vol. 1 p.79 : It is likely that Khushwant Singh was influenced by Ganda Singh (A History of the Sikhs) who gives the date as about 1687, which is nigh impossible as at the time Guru was lodged in Paonta.

[54] A History of the Sikh People by Dr. Gopal Singh – p.275

[55] A History of the Sikhs by Khushwant Singh – Vol. 1 p.81 : Cognizant of the examples of Prithi Chand, Dhirmal and Ram Rai, each of whom disputed the succession and set up as rival gurus, Guru Gobind felt that, notwithstanding he had four sons, a living mentor could be replaced by some institution which discharged the same functions.

According to W.H. McLeod Guru "having reflected on the perils of his situation, and the apparent weakness of his timid followers, had devised a plan whereby to infuse a spirit of strength and unity" ((Sikhs and Sikhism – essay on The Evolution of the Sikh Community p.14).

He summoned his followers from everywhere to descend on Anandpur for the celebration of the 1699 Baisakhi festival and to come "wearing arms and maintaining their beards and hair inviolate".[56]

Baisakhi 1699 was critical turning point in Sikh history, a day thirty-three year old Guru implemented part of his vision. The occasion marked the founding of the Khalsa (order of the pure). The baptismal ceremony of initiation into the brotherhood required volunteer aspirants to shed their caste by adopting the neutral name of Singh (meaning lion), reject old scriptures and places of pilgrimage, disavow worship of Hindu deities, belief in one god, not to cut any bodily hair and instructed on a code of conduct. They also took the vow of unity and loyalty, to fight injustice and not to betray their faith even under cruelest of persecution, activists in the vein of Sant-Sipahi (warrior saint). By the end of the festivities, twenty thousand men were administered baptism and admitted into the Khalsa brotherhood.

Myriads of followers from everywhere, belonging to all castes, gravitated to Anandpur. According to Harbans Singh, "Anandpur became a Mecca for those whose hearts rebelled against inequality and tyranny of the rulers". The place grew and became a hub of armed men. The city pulsated with a new rhythm of religious fervour, maintenance of fortifications and military exercises. The nagara (war drum) beaten twice daily and the sound reverberated through the hills.

---

[56] Guru Gobind Singh by Harbans Singh – p.44

The happenings made the hill chiefs, Raja Ajmer Chand of Bilaspur in particular, jittery and concerned. They concluded they should nip the Guru's growing power in the bud before it was too late. They, therefore, banded together to come up with a strategy to provoke the Guru.

The devious stratagem envisaged by Raja of Bilaspur was to expel the Guru from Anandpur on the grounds of refusal by the Guru to pay rent for the territory he occupied. Guru insisted that he owned the freehold on the territory. The defiance of the Guru provided the Raja with the alibi to order his army to throw a cordon around the city. The Guru escaped to a nearby village of Nirmoh. While Guru was on his way, the Rajah laid ambush. Raja was defeated and Guru punished him by way of having several of his villages plundered.

Realizing the Guru was too strong to handle by them, the hill chiefs appealed to Mogul emperor for assistance. Reinforced by the Mogul contingent from Sirhind and Lahore, the hill rulers besieged Nirmoh. During fierce fighting that took place, on October 8 1700, the Guru broke through the siege finding refuge in Basali, a village about 15 Km southwest of Kiratpur. The Raja pursued the Guru. Clobbered badly the Raja sued for peace, and agreed to allow the Guru to return to Anandpur.[57]

---

[57] A History of the Sikhs by Khushwant Singh – Vol. 1 p.90-91; Guru Gobind Singh by Harbans Singh – p.59-61

The return to Anandpur was, however, short-lived. Hill chiefs could not live down their ignominious defeat at the hands of the Guru. Raja Ajmer Chand of Bilaspur in particular felt chagrined the most and nursed a deep grudge against the Guru. Reared on a whole range of Machiavellian ploys, he made overtures of amity while hatching a plot to assail the Guru.

On December 2 1703, Raja Ajmer Chand attacked Anandpur again. He commanded an allied army of 10,000 men chosen from the armed forces of several of the hill chiefs. Eight hundred Sikhs, on the other hand, defended the town. The defenders launched a pre-emptive strike that threw adversary into disarray, forcing the hill men to retreat.

Driven into abject humiliation Raja Ajmer Chand journeyed to the Deccan to warn Emperor Aurengzeb of the growing power of the Guru, which if unchecked may have serious consequences for the Mogul administration. Emperor who had received similar reports in recent past issued a firman (edict) to subedars (governors) of Sirhind and Lahore "to help the rajas destroy the Khalsa".[58]

During the Diwali festival of 1704, Wazir Khan, the governor of Sirhind, led a large allied force of Mogul and hill chiefs towards Anandpur causing consternation among the townspeople. The Sikh fought valiantly and the toll of the dead mounted on

---

[58] A History of the Sikhs by Khushwant Singh – Vol. 1 p.91

both sides. The allied commander tightened the siege. With each passing day the plight of the Sikhs so deteriorated that some Sikhs wished to leave. The Guru agreed to allow them to go on condition they disowned him as their Guru, which the Sikhs did and put in writing.[59] However, the protracted siege turned so increasingly onerous that the Mogul commander offered safe passage to the Guru if he vacated the city. Cognizant of the serious deprivations suffered by his followers and the near depletion of provisions and water, the Guru evacuated the city. That was the last time thirty-eight year old Guru was to see Anandpur, a place where he had spent thirty years of his life.

He had barely left the city when Guru noted that the allied Mogul forces were in hot pursuit of him. Rearguard engagement gave time to the Guru to reach the seasonal stream called Sirsa that at the time, swollen by the winter rains, was in full flood. Some of Guru's party drowned in the icy waters while those who forded the rivulet separated and scattered in complete disorder. Guru placed his mother, wife, and two younger sons in the custody of a trusted Brahmin servant tasked to escort them to safety. The servant, Gangu, took them under his care to his village. The

---

[59] When these men returned to their villages, "they were upbraided by their families for having forsaken the Guru in the hour of difficulty. Even their womenfolk chafed them for their pusillanimity and offered to exchange their skirts for their men's dress and go out to battle for the Guru" - Guru Gobind Singh by Harbans Singh – p.84

name of village is dissimilar: Gopal Singh names it Kheri whereas Harbans Singh names it as Saheri.[60] Gangu was to betray the whereabouts of Guru's family.[61]

Guru's party reduced to forty Sikhs and his two elder sons took refuge in the village of Chamkaur, about 16 Km south-west of Rupnagar. They hurriedly put up improvised barricades and took positions at strategic points. On December 7 1705, the Mogul forces came thundering into the village and cordoned off the area. Wave after wave, a band of five Sikhs (reminiscent of panj piyare, meaning the 'five beloved') fanned out through the barricades to engage the enemy and certain death.[62] Both of the Guru's older sons, Ajit

---

[60] A History of the Sikh People by Dr. Gopal Singh – p.306; Guru Gobind Singh by Harbans Singh – p.73

[61] Gangu, the servant, managed to take Guru's mother, wife, and two sons to his village. Tempted by the cash and jewelry in the possession of Guru's mother, Gangu betrayed their presence to the Chief of Morinda, a city to the south-west. The Chief took Guru's family into custody and then handed them to Wazir Khan, governor of Sirhind. The governor promised to spare the lives of the sons if they embraced Islam. The boys refused to submit and on the advice of the *qadi* (Islamic judge) Wazir Khan sentenced the boys to be bricked alive. While being encased in brick the walls crumbled.
Finally, on the morning of December 12 an executioner slew them. Agonizing over the deaths of her grandchildren, Mata Gujari (Guru's mother) died in mourning - Guru Gobind Singh by Harbans Singh – p.75

[62] In his footnote at page 308, Gopal Singh mentions: "some say it is these forty martyrs that the Guru blessed as the *Muktas* (the saved ones) mention of whom is made in the Sikh prayer. Bhai Jodg Singh does not agree with this. His contention is that it is

Singh and Jujhar Singh, gave the ultimate sacrifice as they charged with their individual bands. At sunset Guru and just five of his followers remained barricaded. The followers implored Guru to make his escape as they felt that without him fellowship of Khalsa faced harm or extinction. The Guru rejected the idea outright. However, the five Sikh invoked their right as panj piyare to pass Gurmatta (resolution) commanding the Guru to leave. The Guru relented and left in the blackness of night, making his way to Machhiwara, a village about 40 Km east of Ludhiana.

The Mogul troops continued their chase of the Guru and encircled Machhiwara. The Pathan companions of the Guru used subterfuge, bluff to fool the Mogul sentries into believing they were carrying in their palanquin a pir (meaning an 'elder'), and slipped through the cordon. Guru reached Jatpura, a village 50 Km south-west of Ludhiana, and was heartbroken to learn the execution of his two youngest sons.

The heinous and cruel manner of execution of the young boys left everyone in the countryside shocked and numbed. Followers cried out for revenge. Meanwhile, forces of Wazir Khan were closing on the Guru. Devoted followers gathered around the Guru including the Sikhs who had deserted the Guru at Anandpur. The two antagonists faced each other at

---

the 40 deserters of Anandpur who came to battle at Muktsar, shamed by their women folk, and died fighting that earned this title"

the village of Khidrana on December 29 1705. The enemy was resoundingly defeated but at a heavy cost of lives. While surveying the battlefield the Guru counted forty dead Sikhs who had disowned him at Anandpur. He blessed them for having redeemed themselves by their martyrdom.[63] In recognition of their sacrifice, the village named Muktsar (the pool of salvation).

The Guru traveled from village to village, largely inhabited by Jat clans, preaching the gospel. Guru's message resonated across the countryside; people came in multitudes and received baptism. The simplicity of the religious credo sans rituals was a magnet for these sturdy and guileless Jats and they embraced the faith in droves.[64]

---

[63] Blessed by the Guru as *Muktas* (the saved ones), these forty martyr are exemplified and remembered in the Sikh prayer (*Ardas*). Muktsar is a place of pilgrimage attracting the faithful from all over to mark the day of salvation.

[64] "The simple, practical and liberating tenets of the new faith appealed to these freedom-loving people (Jats), alien to metaphysical niceties and sophisticated rituals......So, they received the Guru as well as his precept with open arms" - Guru Gobind Singh by Harbans Singh – p.88

According to Khushwanr Singh: "The bulk of coverts were Jat peasants of the central districts of the Punjab (and) the rise of militant Sikhism became the rise of Jat power in the Punjab" - A History of the Sikhs by Khushwant Singh – Vol. 1 p.89. In addition, at page 93 he writes: "The Guru spent almost a year in the country around Muktsar. The stay was most fruitful, for hundreds of thousands of the Jats of Malwa region accepted baptism and joined the *Khalsa* fraternity".

On the reason why Jats entered the *Panth* (Sikh community) in large numbers, W.H. McLeod believes that the Khatris (the

On January 20, 1706 Guru's traverse brought him to Talwandi Sabo (now called Damdama Sahib, meaning 'breathing place'), where he busied himself with his disciple Mani Singh. He recited from memory sacred writings transcribed by Mani Singh that form the current version of Guru Granth Sahib. He also collected his own writings which were subsequently put together by Mani Singh and entitled Dasven Padsah ka Granth (the Granth of the tenth Guru), distinct from the first or the Adi Granth".[65]

During his sojourn in Damdama Guru got word that ninety-year old Aurengzeb was gravely ill, whereupon the Guru felt the imperative need of going to the Deccan to present a petition in person to the emperor seeking punishing Wazir Khan for the unjust killing of his innocent sons.

He set forth and was in Kolayat in Rajputana (now named Rajasthan) when he heard of Aurengzeb's death in Ahmednagar (in present day Maharashtra).[66]

---

class to which the Guru's belonged) "commonly served as teachers of the Jats. Khatris could be expected to direct their teachings to Jats, and Jats could be expected to respond" - (Sikhs and Sikhism – essay on The Evolution of the Sikh Community p.11).

Patwant Singh writes: "The high-placed urban mercantile Khatri caste was the origin of many of Nanak's and later Guru's disciples and closest associates, while the ranks of the widespread Jat caste of village cultivators came to make up a sizeable proportion of the Sikh community" - The Sikhs by Patwant Singh – p.25

[65] A History of the Sikhs by Khushwant Singh – Vol. 1 p.93-94
[66] There is controversy over the date Aurengzeb died.

Aurengzeb's death in the Deccan was to result in a war of succession. Muazzam (Shah Alam), the older son, who was at the time near Lahore, crowned himself in May 1707, and assumed the title Bahadur Shah. The younger brother Azam Shah who was in Ahmednagar announced himself emperor and hurried towards Agra. However, Muazzam's son, Azim-us-Shan rushed to Agra and besieged the city on behalf of his father. The Guru gave succour to Muazzam in the form of "a detachment of Sikh horsemen".[67] Bahadur Shah, assisted albeit by a small Sikh force, defeated, and killed his pretender brother at the battle of Jajau on June 18, 1707.

The youngest brother to Bahadur Shah, Kam Baksh, governor of Bijapur, had also meanwhile crowned himself emperor on hearing the news of his father's death and mobilized his forces to capture the throne.

Ashirbadilal Srivastava gives the date as March 3, 1701 (The Mogul Empire; p.357)
Harbans Singh believes he died on February 20,1707 (Guru Gobind Singh; p.95)
 Khushwant Singh provides March 2, 1707 (A History of the Sikhs; p.94)
 According to Patwant Singh, the Guru "was in Rajputana in February 1707 when the news of the   emperor's death in Ahmednagar reached him" (The Sikhs; p.66).
The distance between Ahmednagar and Delhi is about 1,100 Km. The fastest way of carrying messages in those days was most likely by horseback riders. Given that a horseman may cover 60 Km a day, it will have taken, a relay of horsemen, about 20 days to deliver the news, which would put the emperor's death in the early days of February as per Patwant Singh.
[67] A History of the Sikhs by Khushwant Singh – Vol. 1 p.94

That prompted Bahadur Shah to leave Agra to subdue his brother. Feeling that he may be able to bring about rapprochement between the brothers, the Guru, and his small band traveled alongside the emperor.

In September 1708, Guru arrived in the town of Nanded, on the banks of Godavari River, and encamped there. Within a month, Guru's Afghan guard stabbed the Guru who died soon after. At his deathbed on October 7, 1708, the Guru declared an end to the line of personal Gurus and charged his followers from henceforth to look upon the Granth as an embodiment of the ten Gurus and consider it as their guide and moral compass.

In last nine years of his life, the Guru had revolutionized the Sikh community. In 1699 he inculcated his followers with a sense of moral life, duty to humankind, and to take up cudgels on behalf of the oppressed and downtrodden i.e. spirit of Sant-Sipahi (warrior saint). Nine years later, in 1708, his vision, and dream materialized when he charged his followers to pay obeisance and reverence to the Granth, which was to be their moral compass for eternity.

In a span of a hundred years a people who were meek and mild had morphed into a fearless and forthright people and a champion of the weak and oppressed. It all began in 1606 when Guru Hargobind, the orphaned son of the martyred Guru Arjun, established Akal Takht, the temporal seat of Sikh power and in 1699 Guru Gobind, the orphaned son of the martyred Guru Tegh Bahadur, strengthened that temporal endowment by the creation of a permanently armed cadre of men to protect and defend the faith.

4 - BANDA BAHADUR: the man, exploits and legacy

Banda Bahadur entered pages of Sikh history with his initiation into the faith, circa September 1708, aged 38; and, exited seven years later, at age 45, when he was savagely put to death. This short span of seven years encapsulates the measure of the man.

A month before Guru Gobind Singh passed away, at Nanded, in early October 1708, he met 38-year-old recluse Madho Das. The Guru knew his reputation as a man of miracles. At their first encounter, Madho Das paid obeisance to the Guru, came forward to receive baptism, and was given name Banda Singh. His courage and indomitable spirit earned him the byname bahadur (the brave), and he came to be known as Banda Bahadur.

Guru Gobind Singh's lament over the cold-blooded killing of his two younger sons rushed out in a palpable wave among all his followers. Guru had expressed his grief in words that "the tyrannous rule (of Mogul) be destroyed, root and branch. The city of Sirhind will be completely ruined, brick clashing with brick".[68]

---

[68] A History of the Sikh People by Dr. Gopal Singh p.341

Guru Gobind then armed Banda Bahadur with "five arrows and an escort of a few chosen Sikhs",[69] entrusted him as "military commander of a punitive expedition"[70] and directed him "to wreak vengeance on the Turk".[71]

Both Ganda Singh and Purnima Dhavan hold an altogether different view. Ganda Singh discounts the idea that Guru Gobind deputed Banda Bahadur as an avenger; instead, he believes, he introduced Banda as a Khalsa "commander". Ms. Dhavan maintains that "within a year of Guru Gobind's assassination" letters, identical to Guru's hukumnamas, bearing the imprimatur of a "mysterious figure called Banda" spread widely in Punjab designating Banda as the chosen representative of the Guru.[72]

Beginning from the times of Guru Hargobind, both the spiritual authority (piri) and temporal authority (miri) rested in the Guru. Now, for the first time,

---

[69] Guru Gobind Singh by Harbans Singh – p.98
[70] A History of the Sikhs by Khushwant Singh – Vol. 1 p.103 – Reason the ascetic was chosen is stated at p101-102, viz., Guru "felt in the spare frame of the ascetic smouldered the Promethean fire which could be fanned into a flame. He summoned Lachman Das and charged him with the duty of punishing the men who had persecuted the Sikhs and murdered his sons. He gave Lachman Das a new name, which the latter had himself chosen to describe his relationship to the Guru – *banda*, or the slave".
[71] *ibid* footnote reference to *Panth Prakash* by Gyani Gyan Singh
[72] When Sparrows Became Hawks: The Making of the Sikh Warrior Tradition 1699-1799 - Oxford University Press, 2011 – page 49

temporal leadership devolved upon not just someone other than a Guru but one little known within the community. That which is unclear is the circumstances that persuaded the Guru to have "chosen a complete stranger to lead the Sikhs".[73]

Banda was "fired by a furious religious zeal and burning spirit of retaliation" and set out to carry out the mission.[74] The size of detachment that Banda led as he left Nanded headed for Punjab is unknown except for mention by George Forster, an East India Company functionary, who left Calcutta in September 1782 and traversed through Benares (present day Varanasi), Allahabad, Lucknow, and Furruckabad. Whilst traveling through Punjab circa 1783 Forster learned that " a Sicque disciple, named Bunda (sic), who had attended Govind Sing (sic), came, after the death of his chief, into the Punjab, where, claiming a merit from his late connection, he raised a small force, and in various desultory enterprises, established the character of a brave but cruel soldier".[75]

---

[73] A History of the Sikhs by Khushwant Singh – Vol. 1 footnote - p.101- p102:"Guru Gobind's choice of Banda in preference to many of his own companions has never been explained. From the chronology of the Guru's travels, it appears that he did not live more than one month in Nanded. It is hardly likely that he would have chosen a complete stranger to lead the Sikhs unless he had known of the man earlier or Banda had already earned the reputation of a leader".
[74] The Sikh Gurus and the Sikh Society by Niharranjan Ray – p.109
[75] A Journey from Bengal to England, Through the Northern part of India, Kashmire (sic) Afghanistan, and Persia and into Russia, by the Caspian Sea by George Forster– printed for R.

A present day journey by road from Nanded to Delhi is 1,390 Km. At the time of Banda's travel roadways were almost non-existent which would mean that his route coursed through villages, wooded tracts and jungles and, therefore, likely more circuitous. It took almost a year for Banda to reach Delhi. The Sikhs of the city who lent him financial support warmly received him and devout Sikhs "abandoned their hearths and homes in their hundreds in Majha, Malwa, and Doaba, and marched out to join Banda's forces".[76]

Before Banda made his presence felt in the Malwa region of Punjab the Sikh peasantry, though a subjugated people, faced little intervention in their daily lives from the ruling class provided they were not militant activist and lived a routine life.

The countryside of Punjab in the eighteenth century was a scattering of villages and towns interconnected by tree lined kacha raasta (dirt roads), and the land endowed with rivers and fresh water aquifers. The rich soil, proximity to rivers and fresh-water aquifers make the land suitable for cultivation and pasture. The Mogul introduced novel methods to enhance the fertility of the soil by setting land aside for particular purpose e.g. 'polaj' (raising two crops every year), 'parauti' (land left fallow after two crops). State

---

Faulder & son in 1808 – page 303. The book is mostly a collection of letters written with a couple of other chapters (e.g. a chapter on Rohillas).
[76] A History of the Sikh People by Dr. Gopal Singh – p.334-335

undertook the construction of canals and reservoirs. The cropping patterns, irrigation facilities, and land management formed basis of a strong economy, prompting Moguls to bring more and more land under cultivation, which "accelerated the sedentarization of formerly nomadic groups such as the Jats, who slowly began to appear more frequently in Mogul sources as prosperous peasants and zamindars (landowners)"[77].

Mogul Punjab boasted of two major cities: Lahore and Multan, both thickly populated. Lahore was a thriving cultural centre of the Mogul Empire, a jewel in its crown. It is located a mile south of the Ravi River and sits on an elevated knoll. It is a citadel city of antiquity being in the direct path of invaders from the north. It was a great and wealthy city; an imperial city much coveted by Mogul ruling class and naturally lusted after by the Sikh misldars (supreme commanders).[78]

Purnima Dhavan relies on the 17th century account by Mobad. In his work Dabistan-i-Mazahib Mobad "present(s) us with a picture of conception of spiritual authority within the (sixth) Guru's family as well as from the perspective of ordinary Sikhs" which is based on his personal interviews with the "sixth and seventh Sikh Gurus as well as a number of Sikhs from

---

[77] When Sparrows Became Hawks: The Making of the Sikh Warrior Tradition 1699-1799 by Purnima Dhavan - Oxford University Press, 2011 – page 27

[78] The Commentary of Father Monserrate, S J On his Journey to the Court of Akbar, published 1922 by Oxford University Press – page 70

diverse backgrounds".[79] Mobad characterizes Guru Hargobind's relations with the Mogul as nebulous. Periodically the Guru "aided the imperial army, his armed retainers also clashed with Mogul commander's forces", leading to surmise by Purnima Dhavan: "long before the creation of the Khalsa, we have the beginnings of an armed group within the Panth and growing opposition to imperial authority".[80]

The Jat peasants and zamindars were heavily concentrated in the tract encompassing Majha and Bist-Doab lying between Ravi River and Sutlej River, and the Malwa region in the Delhi Doab. Many of these Jats may not have formally submitted to Khalsa baptism but they, nevertheless, embraced Khalsa ethos as evident in Guru Arjun bringing "into his fold thousands of Jats of the Majha country, the sturdiest peasants of the Punjab".[81] They lived among hostile rivals comprising Afghans, Ranghar Rajputs and Mogul functionaries. The two factions often found themselves fighting over land and power. The Mughul administration aided the rivals to the great detriment of the peasants.

The peasants were levied a tax equivalent to one-third of the average yield per bigha (a land measure varying from a third of an acre) in respect of every crop. The

---

[79] When Sparrows Became Hawks: The Making of the Sikh Warrior Tradition 1699-1799 by Purnima Dhavan - Oxford University Press, 2011 – page 30
[80] Ibid – page 30
[81] A History of the Sikhs by Khushwant Singh – Vol. 1 p.57

tax collectors tried to exact more than the assessment and these illegal imposts resulted in recurring arrears, often forcing peasants to resort to tax evasions. With the sunset of Mogul rule, the economic situation became so chaotic that powerful nobles established their own "provincial dynasties in several parts of the country" and to sustain their lavish way of life tried to exact much more revenue.[82] This additional levy left many Jats with just enough produce for their own consumption, leaving little or nothing to sell in the market to maintain a decent standard of living. The pressure of subsistence living was another impulse to throw off the yoke of Mogul zamindars.

When the word of Banda's conquests in the Malwa reached the exasperated peasantry, it not only lit a spark of political rebellion in their hearts but also persuaded the Jat peasantry to align with and support Banda Bahadur's rebellion.[83]

A determined force of Malwa peasantry quickly defeated the faujdar at Rahon (a town 20 Km south

---

[82] The Mogul Empire by Ashirbadilal Srivastava – p. 490, p.525
[83] Purnima Dhavan explains Banda evoked Guru Gobind's "memory in multiple ways" to win over the *Jat* peasantry. "Banda's rebellion also visited the sacred geography associated with the last Guru's life, although in reverse, building solid associations with the Guru in popular memory. ......At the very beginning of his rebellion, Banda led a raid on Sirhind. Wazir Khan himself was killed and his body out up for public display, while the town was plundered with ruthless efficiency and destroyed". When Sparrows Became Hawks: The Making of the Sikh Warrior Tradition 1699-1799 by Purnima Dhavan - Oxford University Press, 2011 – page 51

of Garhshankar; 30 Km northeast of Ludhiana) and "seized Jullundur and Hoshiarpur and by the autumn of 1710 liberated the whole of Jullundur Doab".[84] At about the same time, as per Dr. Gopal Singh "the Sikhs of Majha also rose in revolt and with a small irregular force" captured Batala, Kalanaur, and Pathankot and threatened Lahore.[85]

Thus did the Malwa and Majha peasantry not just capture Bist Doab they also overran the tract between the Sutlej and the Ravi, except for Lahore and the Afghan town of Kasur. The peasants seized land owned by Muslim feudal lords and divided the spoils among themselves. There is no evidence indicating Banda personally headed any of the peasant campaigns or that he provided any reinforcements; however, there is little doubt that he was a catalyst and an instrument in stoking up the revolt.

Purnima Dhavan argues that as the Mogul tried to rescue the fragmentation of their administration by appealing to "key Muslim groups in Panjab such as the Afghans, Ranghar Rajputs, and Bhattis" and the Khalsa Sikhs resorted to "similar overtures of support to Jat clans and to other non-Muslim peasant communities in the region". Relations between the two coalitions polarized into two competing ideological positions and "these coalitions attempted to monopolize the military labor and revenue generated by peasant communities, while denying it to

---

[84] A History of the Sikhs by Khushwant Singh – Vol. 1 p.108
[85] A History of the Sikh People by Dr. Gopal Singh p.344

their rivals". Because of the diversity in their ranks, the Khalsa accommodated "a diversity of social practices" that by mid-eighteenth century resulted in a "hybrid Khalsa culture (that) appealed to a wide range of peasant communities in Panjab and also fostered ties with multiple Sikh groups that were not part of the Khalsa community".[86]

The peasant conquests was also made easy as Mogul emperor Bahadur Shah was pre-occupied in subduing the revolt by his brother in the Deccan and planning occupation of Rajasthan. However, the news of the peasant uprising impelled the Emperor to mobilize his forces against the Sikhs under the generalship of Firoz Khan. "By December 1710, Mogul rule was re-established in the Malwa plain".[87]

The peasant revolt fizzled out and land appropriated by the peasants reverted to the Mogul zamindars (landlords). The peasant revolt, therefore, was short-lived.

Banda Bahadur had swept into Punjab with a small band of warriors. His daring rampage through Samana and Sirhind were to impel a large number of Jats and Gujjars to join the rebellion.[88] These tribal

---

[86] When Sparrows Became Hawks: The Making of the Sikh Warrior Tradition 1699-1799 by Purnima Dhavan - Oxford University Press, 2011 – pages 48-49
[87] A History of the Sikhs by Khushwant Singh – Vol. 1 p.110
[88] Banda attracted a very diverse following. Many groups joined him once he had collected enormous wealth from raids on cities such as Samana, Sadhaura, Sirhind, and even Lahore. This loot

people, known for their stubborn streak and ill temper, are esteemed skilful tillers and farmers who raise and breed livestock. Some joined to obtain a protection against the rapacity of Sikh adventurers, others as refuge from the burdensome economic demands of the Mogul rulers while many were enticed to embrace the Khalsa creed from the hope of participating in plunder and pillage. They drew strength from the spirit and valour of Banda who "had inspired them with a zeal, which rendered meritorious every act of cruelty to the enemies of their faith, an irresistible impulse".[89]

As more and more peasants rallied round to his cause, he was able to establish a turbulent presence in the Malwa region. In a brief span of seven years Banda managed to occupy "the country between the Sutlej and Jumna, and he lay waste the district of Saharanpur".[90]

As an astute military strategist, Banda scored decisive victories over Mogul forces. He rampaged through

---

was distributed among his followers. Such social and economic asymmetries between the rebels and their targets have influenced scholars who view Banda's rebellion as a widespread peasant revolt stemming from a feudal suppression of peasants by Moghal gentry - When Sparrows Became Hawks: The Making of the Sikh Warrior Tradition 1699-1799 by Purnima Dhavan - Oxford University Press, 2011 – page 53

[89] A Journey from Bengal to England, Through the Northern part of India, Kashmire (sic) Afghanistan, and Persia and into Russia, by the Caspian Sea by George Forster – Letter XI – pages 311-312

[90] History of the Sikhs by J.D. Cunningham – page 77

Muslim controlled towns and villages leaving behind scenes of desolation and ruin, quite unperturbed the wrath his actions would cause the authorities. The carnage and disorder was an affront to Mogul authority, making their resolve even more stubborn that "the name of a Sicque no longer existed in the Mogul dominion".[91]

On November 26, 1709, Banda Bahadur "fell on Samana to which belonged Jala-ud-Din, the executioner of the ninth Guru, Tegh Bahadur and the two killers of Guru Gobind Singh's young sons, Shashal Beg and Bashul Beg".[92] Despite overwhelmingly outnumbered, the "frenzied followers of Banda" stormed the town and fought on for three days "until all that remained was a heap of smoldering ruins and ten thousand corpses strewn about the streets".[93] According to one account, "pools of blood flowed through its drains, while another places the number killed at 10,000".[94] Similar fate awaited Saharanpur.[95]

---

[91] The Sikh Gurus and the Sikh Society by Niharranjan Ray – p.109
[92] A History of the Sikh People by Dr. Gopal Singh - p.336
[93] A History of the Sikhs by Khushwant Singh – Vol. 1 p.104;
[94] The Sikhs by Patwant Singh – p.71
[95] "It is unnecessary to state the particulars of this memorable incursion, which, from all accounts, appears to have been one of the severest scourges with which a country was ever afflicted. Every excess that the most wanton barbarity could commit, every cruelty that an unappeased appetite of revenge could suggest, was inflicted upon the miserable inhabitants of the provinces through which they passed. Life was only granted to those who conformed to the religion, and adopted the habits

The prosecution of war against the Mogul occupation was relentless and Banda granted Moguls no quarter as manifest in the pillaging in the aftermath of the assault on Samana, which was "in every way much more rewarding (than Kaithal) and of far greater significance. His soldiery received a substantial share of the loot, leaving a sizeable sum also for the future warfare".[96]

Banda attacked several other towns before wreaking havoc on Sirhind. He "punished the city in a vindictive and barbarous manner. He commanded it to be fired and all the inhabitants to be put to death (and) the corpse of Wazir Khan hanged on a tree".[97]

The Mogul emperor directed his imperial forces in relentless pursuit of Banda. The emperor "ordered Abdul Samad Khan, surnamed Idler Jang, a Turani nobleman, governor of Kashmir, and a general of great reputation, to assume the command of the Panjab, and punish the insurgent Banda and his fanatic followers".[98]

The imperial forces pursued Banda doggedly. After several close escapes Banda and his followers took

---

and dress of the Sikhs" – Sketch of the Sikhs by Sir John Malcolm.
[96] A History of the Sikh People by Dr. Gopal Singh - page 335 describes his attitude to robbers; page 337 informs reader of his ironic about-face by engaging in looting.
[97] History of the Punjab by Syed Muhammad Latif published 1891- p.274 –p.275
[98] *Ibid.* -- p.278

refuge in Sadhaura in the lower slopes of Sivalik hills east of Ambala.[99] This time around, Banda came under attack from the imperial forces and allied Hindu hill-chiefs who finally drove him northwards to the fort at Gurdaspur where, again, the imperial army laid its siege; a siege lasting a long time intended to deprive the besieged of all supplies. Thousands of Sikh soldiers died from starvation and disease forcing Banda Bahadur "to surrender on December 17, 1715 and was taken prisoner with 740 followers".[100]

Abdul Samad Khan carted Banda and his followers off to Lahore and then to Delhi where the captives were offered reprieve if they renounced their faith and embraced Islam. None betrayed their Khalsa vows, each choosing death. Banda was subjected to cruelest and most inhuman torture, systematic dismembering that ended in his death in June 1716.

Banda spoke his epitaph at his execution saying that when evil men unleash wickedness then "Providence never fails to raise up a scourge like me to chastise a

---

[99] "Support for Banda fluctuated greatly among the groups mentioned above; the thousands who supported him at the peak of his rebellion were reduced to a few hundred by the time of his capture in 1715. Clearly other factors were at play in motivating different groups to ally with Banda". [Different groups mentioned included Nanakpanyjis (non-Khalsa Sikhs), Banjaras (nomadic tribes) and low-caste groups and Ms Dhavan argues that "it is unlikely that all of these groups saw themselves engaged in a war to protect Khalsa dharma"] - When Sparrows Became Hawks: The Making of the Sikh Warrior Tradition 1699-1799 by Purnima Dhavan - Oxford University Press, 2011 – page 53
[100] The Mogul Empire by Ashirbadilal Srivastava – p. 418

race so depraved; but when the measure of punishment is full then he raises up men like you to bring him to punishment".[101]

Banda's portrayal of himself as the scourge, as one that inflicts severe suffering, vengeance, or punishment remains in sharp contrast with the vows he took at his initiation as member of the Khalsa. One of the key tenets of Khalsa charges the disciple to inspire to do good things and desist from doing bad, and embrace ideal of self-sacrifice for the protection and welfare of others. When he first set foot on Punjab soil Banda carried with him the Khalsa creed. His piety was apparent by the way he handled miscreants drawn to his banner in Delhi. He meted out ruthless punishment to robbers and thugs, and "some of these had even to shake off whatever they had accumulated in their exploits of a whole lifetime".[102] However, the killing fields of Samana, Sirhind and Saharanpur, attesting to indiscriminate slaughter of citizenry, is certification of Banda's betrayal of the instructions of Guru Gobind Singh.[103] He was blithely unconcerned about Guru Gobind Singh's specific exhortation to him, which was to seek out and punish only those guilty of crimes against the Sikhs.[104]

---

[101] A History of the Sikhs by Khushwant Singh – Vol. 1 p.117
[102] *ibid.* p.335
[103] The spirit of sectarianism possessed him – History of the Sikhs by J.D. Cunningham p.79
[104] Banda was charged with "the duty of punishing men who had persecuted the Sikhs and murdered his sons" (A History of the Sikhs by Khushwant Singh – Vol. 1 p.101); "Banda bowed at

From the outset Guru Gobind Singh's mandate to Banda was to "punishing the evildoers and raising the poor and the down-trodden in a spirit of dedication and detachment, with God in the heart, ever and at all times, the Guru's hand will always be at his back".[105] The evildoers were the Mogul executioners of Guru Tegh Bahadur, the faujdar of Sirhind who had the two younger sons of Guru Gobind bricked alive and those Mogul functionaries complicit in these atrocities.[106]

Banda Bahadur was elevated to temporal leadership of the Sikh collectivity by Guru Gobind when dispatched to Punjab.[107] However, Banda widened the scope "to embrace a spiritual ministry as well. Crowds began to flock to his camp (and) women to seek his blessings for their families. He preached sermons and gave benedictions".[108] Here again, Banda showed utter disregard of Guru Gobind's injunction.

---

the Guru's feet and promised to do as he was instructed and never to depart from the path set out for him by the Master" - A History of the Sikh People by Dr. Gopal Singh p.321
[105] *Ibid.* p.321
[106] *Ibid.* p.321 - "march on Sirhind, lay siege to the city and seize and personally execute Wazir Khan, the subedar, whose prosecution the Guru had demanded earlier from the emperor but was disappointed by the latter's evasive replies"
[107] *Ibid.* P.334 - the Guru according to the Sikh chronicles, had instructed Banda "not to forget himself on attaining power" and "to keep chaste and disciplined in war as in peace and not to set himself up above the people, and keep the fear of God and Guru always in mind
[108] A History of the Sikhs by Khushwant Singh – Vol. 1 p.103

To inspire enlisted troops, hone their military skills and foster their combative mood, more so when one is engaged in perpetual warfare is the ethos of military leadership. Even in his role of temporal leadership, Banda Bahadur came up short. For example, his whereabouts from end of 1712 to February 1715 remain shrouded in mystery. During that period of two years his life is blanked out in the chronicles of his times. He appears to have relinquished his temporal leadership and leave his followers sans leader.

His sequestering himself was, therefore, uncharacteristic of a person anointed temporal leader of the community; an abdication of responsibility. His isolation was betrayal of his covenant made with Guru Gobind Singh who blessed him to champion the rights of the poor and downtrodden people struggling for social justice and to remember that as long as he remained god-fearing, the Guru will watch over him.

From an objective and impartial standpoint, Banda had no burning vision inside him to spawn and establish Khalsa raj. He was not a worldly man and he did not fully comprehend the scope of temporal power (concept of 'miri' dealing with governance). He was primarily a warrior, a soldier par excellence.

Banda left behind no written word to judge him by. Instead, historians who have weighed in with varying degree of editorialized commentary tell his story. No matter how diligently a reader trawls through the narrative of these historians he cannot help notice not just inconsistencies in their accounts but also paucity of information.

Banda's birthplace is in dispute.[109] There is also disagreement over his upbringing. According to Khushwant Singh Banda "joined an order of bairagi (mendicants) at an early age and was given a new name, Madho Das. He went south and spent many years in Hindu monasteries in Central India".[110] On the other hand, Gopal Singh explains that Banda "farmed for some time, practiced firearms and went on hunting expeditions; and, that his killing a pregnant deer so traumatized him that "he renounced the world and became a recluse, settling later at Nanded".[111]

These inconsistencies aside, the accounts of the historians fall short of the conventions of normal chronology.

Dates of some key events are obscure.[112] There is also an unexplained lacuna in Banda's story. Two years of

---

[109] J.D. Cunningham writes that Banda "the chosen disciple of Gobind, was a native of the South of India" - History of the Sikhs; p.77. Khushwant Singh maintains that Banda was born in 1670 at Rajauri (Poonch) - A History of the Sikhs; p.101). And Gopal Singh attests that Banda was born in Poonch, near Rajauri (Kashmir) - A History of the Sikh People; p.320
[110] A History of the Sikhs by Khushwant Singh – Vol. 1 p.101 footnote
[111] A History of the Sikh People by Dr. Gopal Singh p.320
[112] The date Banda arrived in Delhi is unclear. Khushwant Singh, at page 102, simply writes "Banda left the Deccan with a small

his life remain un-chronicled. Driven out of Sadhaura and Mukhlisgar by the Mogul armies towards the end of 1712, Banda found refuge in a village near Jammu (now known as Dera Baba Banda). In February 1715, he "came down from his mountain retreat to measure his sword again with the Moguls".[113] That encounter was fated to end in his capture and brutal death.

Intriguingly, history makes no mention of Banda visiting Harminder Sahib, Sikhdom's spiritual centre or that he availed himself of the opportunity to take the platform at Akal Takht, seat of temporal authority, to send out a rallying call to Sikhs to rid Punjab of Mogul rule.

Some historians claim that the military successes caused Banda to be afflicted with hubris and "building a personality cult around him".[114]

---

band and came northwards (and) planted the Guru's standard in a village thirty-five miles from the capital and forwarded the Guru's letter ordering the Sikhs to join him". Dr. Gopal Singh, at pages 334-335, states "Banda took nearly a year to reach the Panjab (and) on his way to the Panjab, he was met with in Rajputana as also in and round Delhi by men of his faith". Then again, the date Banda left Delhi and set off on his campaign to Sirhind is unknown. According to Khushwant Singh, at page 103-104, "Banda left the neighbourhood of Delhi and traveled northwards along the Grand Trunk Road" whereas Dr. Gopal Singh, at page 336, describes the strategy adopted by Banda to capture Sirhind.

[113] A History of the Sikhs by Khushwant Singh – Vol. 1 p.112-113
[114] A History of the Sikh People by Dr. Gopal Singh – p.355

Lt.-Col Malcolm believes Sikhs encouraged by Banda's successes followed him to the field. However, they do not revere his memory as he is termed a heretic who "endeavored to change the religious institutions and laws of Guru Govind, many of whose devoted followers this fierce chief put to death, because they refused to depart from those usages which that revered spiritual leader had taught them to consider sacred". Instead of exclaiming the traditional wahe Guru ji ka khalsa, wahi Guru ji ki fateh he directed his followers to exclaim "Futteh D'herm! Futteh dershan! which means 'success to piety! success to the sect".[115]

Another pivotal moment that captures Bandas hubris involves the overture made by the Mogul emperor Farukh-Siyar to Mata Sundri, the widow of Guru Gobind Singh. The emperor chose Bhai Nand Lal "to intercede on his behalf with Banda" to promote reconciliation between "the Hindu hill chiefs and the Guru's house". Greatly incensed at the intervention of Mata Sundri, Banda's insolence is manifest in his reply that "I am no longer your Sikh, but a Bairagi and a Vaishnava".[116]

Sikh historians write glowingly about Banda, the quintessential military tactician, an abolitionist of zamindari (land-owning families), a man who shook

---

[115] Sketch of the Sikhs by Lt.-Col Malcolm published 1812 – p.83 – p.84
[116] a quote from Prachin Panth Prakash in A History of the Sikh People by Dr. Gopal Singh – p.347

the Mogul empire; and glorify his victorious campaigns against Mogul authorities and his enduring a tortuous death with great fortitude. Muslim historians, Syed Muhammad Latif in particular, portray Banda as an enemy of Islam, someone remembered as a "monster" for his "malicious and cold-blooded atrocities".[117]

The Muslim historians accused of making "vicious attacks on the character of Banda" are dismissed as "mostly courtiers of the empire or in the imperial pay".[118] Latif, a Muslim and a recognized doyen of Indian historians, does not fit that mould. However, in spite of his accusatory view, Dr. Gopal Singh admits grudgingly that Banda caused "much devastation of village and town" and that "blood flowed in torrents and excesses must have been committed by Banda and his men to settle scores of a whole century of persecution and humiliation".[119]

Lt-Col. Malcolm portrayed Banda Bahadur thus: "though a brave and able leader, was one of the most cruel and ferocious of men, and endeavored to pass to his followers that feeling of merciless resentment which he cherished against the whole Muhammedan race".[120]

---

[117] History of the Punjab by Syed Muhammad Latif published 1891 p.280
[118] A History of the Sikh People by Dr. Gopal Singh – p.356
[119] *ibid.* – p. 354
[120] Sketch of the Sikhs by Lt.-Col Malcolm published 1812 – p.82

67

While acknowledging Banda's savagery Sikh historians have eulogized his accomplishments.[121] Exaggerations abound in their measure of the man. Patwant Singh claims that Banda established an independent Sikh state but with nothing to substantiate his statement.

Its borders that are not transitory define a nation state. There is no disputing that Banda swept through several towns and villages controlled by the Mogul ruling class. His campaign, however, was limited to the Malwa region and even therein, his major forays into Samana, Sirhind, Ghuram, Shahabad, Mustafabad, and Sadhaura circumscribed roughly within 50 Km radius of Ambala.[122] That area does not represent vast swathes of the Malwa region.

The farthest incursion to the east was the sacking of Saharanpur, a town across Jamna River, in present day Uttar Pradesh, that lies about 80 Km from Ambala. His involvement in taking of Jullundur and Hoshiarput is unproven but even if conceded Hoshiarpur is situated about 190 Km and Jullundur city about 170 Km from Ambala. That area does not

---

[121] Banda and his men had wrested extensive territories from the paramount power to establish first ever independent Sikh state complete with its royal seal (The Sikhs by Patwant Singh; p.81); Banda made his people taste the fruits of political freedom (A History of the Sikh People by Dr. Gopal Singh; p.355); Banda changed the class structure of land holdings in the southern half of the state by liquidating many of the big Muslim zamindar (land-owning) families of Malwa and the Jullundur Doab (A History of the Sikhs by Khushwant Singh; p.118)
[122] A History of the Sikhs by Khushwant Singh p.105

represent a significant portion of Bist Doab. That said there is no reliable data to indicate he ever crossed Beas River into the Majha region.

Furthermore, the path to his territorial triumphs begin with the sacking of Samana in November 1709, ending in the fall of 1710 with the seizure of Jullundur and Hoshiarpur, a period roughly nine months long; an indication that Banda staged lightning raids. The swathes of land in question were fleetingly possessed and, therefore, does not jibe with Patwant Singh's assertion that Banda Bahadur had "wrested extensive territories" from the Mogul power. Still, this was all for naught as, according to Khushwant Singh, "by December 1710 Mughul rule was re-established in the Malwa plains".[123]

Can it be said that Banda made "his people taste the fruits of political freedom" as argued by Khushwant Singh.

As noted earlier, the peasant uprising led to seizure and redistribution of land but the euphoria soon wore out as the imperial forces restored the land to the Mogul nobles. Even though the rapture was brief, the peasants learned what it means to enjoy political freedom. The claim that Banda "abolished the corrupt and extortionist intermediaries, called the Zamindars (absentee landlords) and distributed land to the tillers of the soil" remains substantially unproven.[124]

---

[123] A History of the Sikhs by Khushwant Singh p.110
[124] A History of the Sikh People by Dr. Gopal Singh p.342

Banda died in June 1716 and it was not until Baisakhi day 1733 that various Sikh bands (Jathas) were organized into the Buddha Dal and the Taruna Dal. During this period of nearly seventeen years, the Sikh collectivity was not just without a temporal leader but was out in the wilderness. No one filled the vacuum or take up the cudgels on behalf of the Sikh collectivity, making legacy of Banda less than enduring.

When all is said and done, Banda was single-minded in his determination "to punish the Turk" to avenge the brutal murder of Guru Gobind's father and young sons. His sledgehammer annexation of Muslim controlled towns and villages unhinged the Mogul empire. These deeds made his name synonymous with terror. In addition, the aura of audacity about him won him acclaim for his bravery and stratagems. His enthusiastic followers exalted him above mere mortals, which according to Dr. Gopal Singh promoted "a personality cult around him". As the volume of kudos ratcheted up, Banda succumbed to hubris and came to assume the mantle of piri (spiritual leadership) of the Sikh people as well. To Sikhs who had accepted Granth Sahib (Sikhdom's holy book) as the final and eternal Guru, as instructed by Guru Gobind, Banda had committed a sacrilege.

In the face of death, Banda Bahadur redeemed himself. The Mogul ruler offered to spare his life if he embraced Islam and renounced his Sikh faith. He refused to betray the religion of the Sikh Gurus. He was dismembered limb by limb, his eyes "cut out of their sockets", his torso "torn by red-hot pincers" and yet he "bore his tortures with utmost equanimity and poise of mind and soul".[125]

Whereas Pancho Villa in death bears a public memory that is burnished and gloriously expanded and his wrongdoings as a bandit and outlaw a mere footnote in history, that Banda in death remembered as an avenger is an irony. His story makes a sorry epitaph: "devoid of all the better qualities of his illustrious predecessor (Guru Gobind Singh), Banda had nothing to commend his memory to posterity, save an undaunted spirit".[126]

---

[125] A History of the Sikh People by Dr. Gopal Singh p.353
[126] History of the Punjab by Syed Muhammad Latif published 1891- p.281

5 – THE IDEA OF MISL, evolution and sphere of influence

Banda Bahadur left behind a mixed legacy. During his eight years of rebellion, he had attracted a diverse following, in later years increasingly from devout Khalsa, and his personal magnetism was the basis of his commanding influence over them. But towards the end of his life the notion of a single temporal leader was beginning to clash with the Khalsa creed of sovereignty of Panj Piare (governance by a body corporate made of five baptized Sikhs). Many of Banda's followers who had served under his banner for eight years were becoming aware that Banda "did not wholly imbibe the spirit of which the Gurus had invested the whole people with sovereignty, also making each of the constituents a full and equal partner in spiritual hope as much as in social and political ascendancy"[127].

Following Banda's death a few individuals jockeyed to make a power grab but no one was able to fill the deep void of leadership and the Sikh community grappled with the religious imperative of temporal leadership. In the meantime, the fervent followers of Banda Bahadur found themselves not just leaderless but also penniless and with an uncertain future. These zealots kept alive the cult of Banda and started to call

---

[127] A History of the Sikh People by Dr. Gopal Singh p.355

themselves Bandais, which created a schism in the Sikh faith. They remembered the battles they waged against the Mogul satraps and of enriching themselves with spoils. Marauding for them had become a way of life. The ecstasy of triumphs and freebooting was, therefore, their motivation to form their own Jathas (gangs).

At the time, divisions within the Sikh community ran deep. On societal level, the community was fragmented into minor sects such as Gulab Raias (followers of Gulab Rai, a cousin of Guru Gobind Singh), Gangu Sahias (followers of Gangu, a disciple of Guru Amar Das), and the Handalias (followers of Handal, also a disciple of third Guru).[128] On the religious plane, the Panth (Sikh collectivity) was divided between Tat Khalsa (orthodox followers of Guru Gobind Singh) led by Kahan Singh, and Bandais, the radical followers of Banda led by Mahant Singh and Lahora Singh Kalal.

On Diwali day in 1720 a quarrel between Tat Khalsa and the Bandais erupted over the division of income of Harminder Sahib that led to open skirmishes on the grounds of the holy temple.[129] This infighting on

---

[128] A History of the Sikhs by Khushwant Singh – Vol. 1 p.122
[129] A History of the Sikh People by Dr. Gopal Singh p.359-360
Purnima Dhavan argues that after the capture of Banda Khalsa Sikhs had "begun actively seek control of Sikh shrines (and that) some of his (Banda) followers continued to occupy the shrine at Amritsar and demanded a share in its offerings" – When Sparrows Became Hawks: The Making of the Sikh Warrior Tradition 1699-1799 page 75

hallowed grounds so dismayed Mata Sundri that she deputed Bhai Mani Singh, in 1721, to take charge of Harminder Sahib and to end factionalism. The internecine rivalry was resolved at a large gathering in Amritsar – a meeting spawning a new genre of meetings that came to be known as Sarbat Khlasa - under whose "instructions Jathedars (chiefs of organized bands) formed small bands of Sikh outlaws and began taking villages near their mountain and jungle hideouts under their protection".[130]

As an outstanding Sikh leader, a brave warrior "held in high esteem on account of his pure life and his commitment to Sikhism"[131], Kapur Singh was recognized as the leader of the Sikhs on Baisakhi day 1733.[132] He was to merge the various Sikh bands (Jathas) into "a central fighting force consisting of two divisions": the Buddha Dal commanded by himself and the Taruna Dal consisting of a number of youthful Jathedars.[133]

In October 1745 the "Sarbat Khalsa resolved to merge the small Jathas into twenty-five sizable regiments", confirmed "Kapur Singh as overall commander of the army" and named some of the regimental commanders: Hari Singh Bhangi, Naud

---

[130] A History of the Sikhs by Khushwant Singh – Vol. 1 p.122
[131] Sardar Jassa Singh Ahluwalia by Ganda Singh – p..9
[132] A History of the Sikhs by Khushwant Singh – Vol. 1 p.122- p.123; The date is in dispute as, according to Seetal, at page 51, Kapur Singh succeeded to the leadership of the *Panth* (Sikh collectivity) on the demise of Diwan Darbara Singh in July 1734
[133] *ibid* - p.123- p.124

Singh of Sukerchak, Jassa Singh Ahluwalia, and Jai Singh Kanhaya.[134]

The reorganized Jathas enjoyed considerable degree of latitude. Each Jatha had its own leader whose followers were beholden to no one but his leader. The leader was conferred the honorific 'sardar', etymology of the word is Persian (from 'sar' which literally means 'head' and 'dar' meaning 'holder').

Each Jatha was an independent unit that could undertake an expedition or go to war under its own leadership so long as the spoils "were distributed in proportion to the strength of each band".[135] They were free to operate as they wished with the sole caveat that they had to merge their units in the Dal Khalsa when the "future of the community was in jeopardy".[136]

In January-February 1746, a Jatha led by Sukha Singh of Marikambo locked horns with Jaspat Rai, Faujdar of Emnabad, over vacating the area where the Jatha had taken shelter. A battle ensued during which one Nibab Singh chopped the head of Jaspat Rai who happened to be a brother of Lakhpat Rai, Diwan of the province of Lahore.

Lakhpat Rai flew into a maddening rage and vowed "eliminating the Singhs" and persuaded Yahya Khan,

---

[134] *ibid* – p.128- p.129
[135] A History of the Sikh People by Dr. Gopal Singh p.385
[136] A History of the Sikhs by Khushwant Singh – Vol. 1 p.123

the Governor of Lahore, to issue "a proclamation for a general massacre of all Sikhs".[137]

In June 1746 the Mogul army "scoured the entire countryside in search of Sikhs" and "hounded (them) out of their hide-outs" forcing some to escape to the hills and jungles while chasing others across Sutlej at Aliwal into Malwa.[138] About 7000 Sikhs were slaughtered in this campaign and another 3000 were put to death by torture and their "heads were piled up to make pyramids" at a place now known as Shaheed Ganj – a disaster etched in Sikh history as ghallughara (the holocaust).[139]

Thus, a purblind Jatha, pledged to one master, was the cause of this horrific ghallughara, a freelance Jatha that flatly failed or refused to see the havoc their actions would wreak on the larger community.

The invasion of India by Ahmad Shah Abdali in 1748 was the turning point giving impetus to these loosely knit Jathas to assume some form of confederacy. An understanding of the circumstances surrounding the invasion will better explain the tie in between the invasion and budding confederacy.

It all began when Shah Nawaz wrested governorship of Lahore from his brother Yahya Khan. In order to strengthen his hold on the governorship he invited

---

[137] Sardar Jassa Singh Ahluwalia by Ganda Singh – p.35
[138] A History of the Sikh People by Dr. Gopal Singh p.379
[139] *ibid* - p.380

Ahmad Shah Abdali, ruler of Afghanistan, to invade India. In the summer of 1747, Abdali entered India in what was the first of Abdali's nine invasions. In March 1748, the Mogul army led by Prince Ahmad Shah, son of Emperor Muhammad Shah, faced Abdali at Manupur, near Sirhind, and "defeated and compelled (Abdali) to retire to Kabul".[140] During Abdali's retreat to Kabul, Sikh Jathas, once again, "appeared on the plains and to start their guerilla activities"; harried and looted his baggage.

General disarray had overtaken the Lahore administrators following the defeat of Abdali, and their ouster was in the offing. Anticipating change of administration in Lahore, "Khalsa Dal held a convention and decided to liberate Amritsar" from the control of Slabat Khan; and tasked Jassa Singh Ahluwalia to attack Amristar. In the ensuing battle both Slabat Khan and his nephew Nazabat Khan were slain and "seeing the dead bodies of their leaders lying on the ground, the army of Slabat Khan lost heart and left the battlefield" and the Singhs established control over Amritsar.[141]

The victorious Sikhs arrived in Amritsar to celebrate Baisakhi 1748 and at a meeting of Sarbat Khalsa resolved to merge the sixty-five independent Jathas into one army, the Dal Khalsa divided into eleven misls with own name, leader and flag, under the

---

[140] The Mogul Empire by Ashirbadilal Srivastava – p. 425
[141] Sardar Jassa Singh Ahluwalia by Ganda Singh – p.52 –p.53

supreme command of Jassa Singh Ahluwalia.[142] The twelfth misl was the Phulkian misl but it was not an integral part of the Dal Khalsa.

The map below illustrates the sphere of influence of the various misls. Bhangi was the most powerful misl, controlling much of the political and economic geography of Punjab. The Bhangis encircled Sukerchakia in the west, east, and north. Phulkia, Shahid, Karorasinghia, and Nishanwalia misl occupied Malwa region.

Several other misls subsisted in the Cis-Sutlej region.

---

[142] A History of the Sikh People by Dr. Gopal Singh p.383 – p.384

The topography of Cis-Sutlej that is encased within Sutlej and Jamna Rivers places it outside of Punjab, a territory mutually carved out among themselves by the misladrs of Patiala, Jind, Nabha, Faridkot, Karorasinghia, Shahid, and Nishanwalia. Most prominent amidst them was the sardar of Phulkian misl located in Patiala.

However, a few other chiefs (Sikh, Hindu, and Muslim) flourished in Punjab. A British administrator and diplomat amply sketched a biography of these second-tier chiefs and families of note.[143]

The misls "were distinguished by titles derived from the name, the village, the district, or the progenitor of the first or most eminent chief or some peculiarity of custom or leadership".[144] The founders of the pre-eminent misls, except Phulkian, originated from villages near Lahore or Amritsar.[145] They were men of humble origins who belonged to farming stock known as zamindars (peasant proprietors). They were generally unsophisticated and unlettered but gifted with innate machismo, religious devotion, and

---

[143] The Punjab Chiefs by Sir Lepel H. Griffin, first published in 1865
[144] History of the Sikhs by J.D. Cunningham - p.96
[145] History of the Punjab by Syed Muhammad Latif published 1891(Chapter iv) - Chajja Singh (misl Bhangi) was native of Panjwar, eight miles from Amritsar; Jai Singh (misl Kanhaya) of village Kanha, 15 miles east of Lahore; (Ahluwalia misl) village of Ahlu, five kos to the east of Lahore; Khosal Singh (Ramgarhia misl) in the vicinity of Amritsar; Kalu, a Hindu Jat (Sukerchakia misl) lived 40 or 50 miles south-west of Lahore

uncanny ability to lead people. They were respected but feared.

Among the eleven misls belonging to Dal Khalsa the five that left lasting footprints of their exploits are Bhangi, Sukerchakia, Kanhaya, Ramgharia, and Ahluwalia. Of them Bhangi misl was the most prominent and powerful until twitched by infighting that provided scions of Sukerchakia misl the opportunity to emasculate the misl.

The misls thrived on plundering of traders, peddlers of wares and convoys of bullock or horse carts engaged in transport of crops, grains, household goods, and wares. Such raids were a regular feature of the second half of eighteenth century, seriously affecting economic activity in Punjab. Lawlessness was so rampant that neither the Mogul nor Sikh leadership could bring it under control.[146] It was only towards the end of the century before the misls metamorphosed into a more responsive system of governance. Moreover, the beginning of this transformation, late in developing, coincided with the waning of the Afghan and Mogul hegemony over Punjab. The popularized belief that the misls governed territories between Jhelum and Sutlej from their inception is not a verifiable claim.

---

[146] When Sparrows Became Hawks: The Making of the Sikh Warrior Tradition 1699-1799 page 62

Lahore, incorporating Punjab, was one of fifteen provinces into which Mogul Empire was divided headed by sipah salar (popularly known as subedhar) assisted by a diwan (akin to a treasury secretary). Each province was divided into sarkars (i.e. districts) headed by a faujdar; each sarkar was divided into parganas; and, each pargana consisted of mouzas which in turn were made up of one or more villages.

Mogul administration was, therefore, well entrenched. Appointed functionaries were responsible to govern, direct, control, and regulate affairs of the people of a village, town, district, or region. They oversaw wellbeing of the people, enforced law and order, built canals and roads, collected taxes and so forth.

The misl leaders neither owned nor ruled over any territory in Punjab. They had carved between themselves spheres of control, an area within which each misl was free to make forays to pillage. Therefore, to all intents and purposes, they were engaged in plain banditry except when the Sikh collectivity was in harm's way and they summoned before the Sarbat Khalsa to unite for a common cause or against a common foe. This dual role made the misl leaders bandit-warriors.

6 - RISE AND FALL OF MISLS, intra and inter misl rivalries

The Afghan invader Ahmad Shah Abdali and his successors repeatedly invaded Punjab intent upon establishing Afghan hegemony in Punjab during the period 1747 to 1799; a period that also epitomizes the emergence, rise, and decline of misl power in Punjab.

The Afghans kept "the Panjab in a state of suspended animation (and) a story of attack and counter-attack, defeat and victory, and insecurity and confusion most of the time".[147]

During this prime time of fifty years, the misls fought on two fronts. They challenged one another over spoils and territory on one front while near simultaneously battling the Afghan invader on the other front. The upshot of these two fronts dictated the ebb and flow of misl hegemony over Punjab.

Following the death of Banda Bahadur, his followers went in many directions to start afresh on their own. Most of them had spent a good deal of life in the Deccan plateau serving Guru Gobind Singh; and, therefore, had become disconnected from their native village. These men were generally illiterate, without

---

[147] The Sikh Gurus and the Sikh Society by Niharranjan Ray – p.112

vocation and lacked the wherewithal to support themselves. They had lived a life of pillage under Banda Bahadur and that was to be their modus operandi going forward.

An unexpected and unasked-for set of circumstances was to boost their chosen way of life of plunder. From 1747 until 1797, the Afghan kings serially invaded India returning to Kabul with untold amount of riches. During same period Punjab was a scene of many battles fought among the Moguls, Afghans, and Marathas for hegemony over Punjab. These turbulent times facilitated guerilla activities of the misldars. They would descend the plains from their hill-hideouts to loot and plunder.

Pillaging skills that the Jathas honed over the years helped them to pounce on the booty-laden Afghan caravan, hit and grab as much of loot and make a getaway to their strongholds and bulwarks in the hills and jungles; redoubts built for better securing their persons and property against Afghan and Mogul search parties.

The amount of loot varied from Jatha to Jatha. The haul of the foxier, brave, competent, energetic, and gifted Jatha leader was comparatively greater than the less skillful leader.

Therefore, richer the plunder of a particular Jatha, more that band was able to attract legion of followers from everywhere. The main criterion for membership was the possession of a horse, equestrian skills, and a fighting spirit. The notion of livelihood dependant on loot and plunder appealed to the men accustomed to sustenance farming. These followers in turn recruited others from family circles, relatives and trusted villagers to join the gang.

Jathas pillaged villages and soon discovered that the villagers felt that with the weakening of Mogul control over Punjab their security of life or property and wellbeing was at risk. They, therefore, developed a new strategy of offering protection to the people. Instead of robbing villagers with use of force as was their practice in the past they now promised to halt future violence in return for a defined sharing of their harvests, a form of forced tithe; and, began seizing villages from Mogul functionaries incrementally and establish their own rule.

Emboldened by their conquests, the misl leaders broadened their horizons. Each secretly dreamed to wrest control of Lahore from Mogul rule, wishing to free the land of their Gurus from the hands of foreign rulers. These aspirations were for naught, thwarted by personal rivalries and strategic interests that exposed deep fractures between the misls. There was a sincere quest for unity but the frequent in-fighting put a damper on the initiatives.

Fighting strength of misls is dubious, variously quantified for some, while for others contrastingly described as "numerous" or "numbered thousands" or "a large force". Latif puts Bhangi misl strength at 20,000 horsemen; Dallewalia between 7,500 and

10,000 strong; Singhpuria around 2,500. Seetal believes Ramgarhia was able to muster 10,000 horsemen.

To put these figures into perspective consider when Babar crossed the River Indus in December 1525 during his fifth and final invasion of India he was "at the head of only 10,000 chosen horses. He marched upon Delhi with an army of 13,000 horse and was met at Panipat by Ibrahim Lodi, at the head of 100,000 horse and 100 elephants" and totally routed Lodi.[148]

Inequity in sharing of plunder and campaigns to extend territorial influence intensified rivalry and political maneuverings among the misldars. Discord was, therefore, inevitable and became a perennial issue both within the misl and between the misls. There was no love lost between the misldars. Shifting alliances made matters worse, prompting some misldars to invite their counterparts to launch an attack on a belligerent chieftain with whom they had a falling-out. They double-crossed each other and often aligned themselves with the enemy (Moguls or Afghans), without compunction.

Such factionalism was the cause of the collateral ebbing away of the strength of some misls, mergers between some others or simply fading away of yet others. Through this prism of hostility and discord

---

[148] History of the Punjab by Syed Muhammad Latif published 1891 – p.124

can be seen the fate of the leading misls and behaviour of the prominent misldars.

Both aspects of inter-misl and intra-misl conflict can best be illustrated through glimpses of the history of leading misls, wherein the depth and intensity of their feuds and quarrels and each key incident of their infighting is sketched.

Bhangi Misl

Chhaja Singh founded the Bhangi misl and was initiated Khalsa of the Guru by Banda Bahadur. Chhaja Singh hailed from village Panjwar, about 13 Km south of Amritsar. Those who knew him revered him. He baptized three of his relatives among them Bhim Singh of Kasur, a town 50 Km south of Lahore. They became comrades in arms engaged in pillage and loot. They in turn baptized several other men and conscripted them into their gang for the purpose of "marauding excursions" and the "armed ruffians began to make night attacks upon villages, carrying away everything of value".[149]

Soon several other sardars from neighboring villages teamed up with them, prominent among them Gurbaksh Singh of village Roranwala (15 Km southeast of Lahore).[150] Gurbaksh Singh owned about forty villages and known widely. Being childless, his heirs were Lehna Singh, an adopted son, and Gujjar Singh, his daughter's son. Both Lehna and Gujjar were the most powerful misldars of the Bhangi confederacy.

As word of the exploits of Bhangis spread, sardars from afar joined the band (e.g. Sahib Singh of Sialkot,

---

[149] History of the Punjab by Syed Muhammad Latif published 1891 p.296 and The Sikh Misls & the Panjab State by Sohan Singh Seetal p.10- p.11
[150] while Sohan Singh Seethal indicates Gurbaksh Singh as a native of Roranwala, Latif at page 300 states his originating from Aura

a town about 300 Km northeast of Lahore; and, Amar Singh of Kingra, a village 152 Km south-west of Ferozpur).

On succeeding Chhaja Singh, Bhim Singh was to integrate the slightly over twenty loosely knit groups into a single misl. The misl derives its name Bhangi from the habit of some of the leading lights who were addicted to Bhang (cannabis sativa).

At their prime time Bhangi enjoyed by far the greatest territorial range than areas under most other misls combined. For instance, entire region between Jhelum and Chenab (i.e. Chaj Doab); most of land between Chenab and Ravi (Rechna Doab) except for the region between Gujrat and Sargodha under Sukerchakia control; Lahore-Amritsar region between Ravi and Beas (Bari Doab).

The consolidated Bhangi misl could mobilize a force of twenty thousand horsemen. All its sardars had equal footing except Gujjar Singh and Lehna Singh of Rattangarh who were a cut above others. On Bhim Singh's death leadership devolved upon his nephew, Hari Singh, who was instrumental in vastly expanding the sphere of Bhangi control.

Harassed by the Sikh misldars during his seventh invasion of India in 1764, Ahmad Shah Abdali feared Sikh Jathas would waylay him while homeward bound. The Baluch overlord Nasir Khan assured Abdali that he and his proxies that included Ala Singh, chief of Phulkian misl, would take care of the annoying Sikhs.[151] As a token of appreciation, Abdali bestowed upon Ala Singh the Governorship of Sirhind.

All of the other eleven misldars, members of Dal Khalsa, were outraged that Ala Singh "had sided with a foreign tyrant"; consequently, the Dal Khalsa army declared war on the Phulkian misl, attacking Patiala in December 1764. Hari Singh, chieftain of Bhangi misl, died on the battlefield. To prevent a dynastic war that would be ruinous for the confederacy, Jassa Singh Ahluwalia, commander of Dal Khalsa army, solved the impasse by having Ala Singh beg forgiveness for his lapses.[152]

With the passing of Hari Singh, Bhangi misl segued into a confederacy, an alliance of three leading sardars: Ganda Singh, Gujjar Singh of Rattangarh and Lehna Singh, among whom Ganda Singh remained by far the most dominant. The relationship between the latter two was a tangle of confusion and difficulty.

Hari Singh had held one Gurbaksh Singh in high esteem by virtue of him being his most trusted and heroic commanders. Gurbaksh Singh fathered a daughter but had no son of his own. He adopted Lehna Singh, a Jat of Saddhawala, as his son and heir-apparent. Gujjar Singh was Gurbaksh Singh's

---

[151] A History of the Sikhs by Khushwant Singh – Vol. 1 p.159
[152] The Sikh Misls & the Panjab State by Sohan Singh Seetal p.13- p.14

grandson by his daughter, Lehna's nephew so to speak.

Jhanda Singh succeeded his father Hari Singh and did not shy away from taking sides in disputes of others. In 1774, Jhanda Singh came to the aid of Raja Ranjeet Dev, ruler of Jammu, an ally, and tributary, whose rebellious son Brij Raj Dev was set to unseat his father. Jhanda Singh was peeved that Kanhaya chieftain Jai Singh and Sukerchakia leader Charat Singh had lined up to support the son. Jhanda Singh marched on Jammu with a large army and a fierce battle followed during which Sukerchakia misldar Charat Singh died after accidentally shooting himself. During the battle, one of his own followers bribed by Jai Singh, the Kanhaya chieftain, assassinated Jhanda Singh.[153]

On succeeding his brother as chief of Bhangi misl, Ganda Singh swore to avenge the murder of his brother. The situation became toxic when the widow of Nand Singh, a Bhangi chief who held the estate of Pathankot – as a gift from Jhanda Singh Bhangi - offered the estate in dowry on the marriage of her daughter to the son of the Kanhaya misl chief. Fully aware of the fallout Kanhaya chief turned down the offer, and instead persuaded Tara Singh, another notable Kanhaya leader to accept the marital arrangement.

---

[153] History of the Punjab by Syed Muhammad Latif published 1891- p.298; The Sikh Misls & the Panjab State by Sohan Singh Seetal – p.21

Thereupon Ganda Singh demanded transfer of the estate back to him; and, the widow refused to give in. The Bhangi chief was outraged. He sought the counsel of Ramgarhia chief Jassa Singh who spurred the Bhangi chief to seek swift retribution and promised his full support. The Bhangi and Ramgarhia forces met the combined forces of Kanhaya, Sukerchakia and Ahluwalia misls at Dina Nagar. During the course of the battle (circa 1774) that lasted many days the Bhangi chief fell ill and died. Since Ganda Singh's son Desa was a minor, Charat Singh, a nephew, assumed the leadership of the Bhangis. In one of the encounters, Charat Singh died in the battlefield of Pathankot and the Bhangi forces retreated.[154]

The Bhangi leadership this time around devolved on Desa Singh, the minor son of Ganda Singh, while Gujjar Singh of Rattangarh appointed a regent. That did not sit well with some proud misldar leaders who had served under storied Bhangi leaders Hari Singh and Ganda Singh and who were not prepared to take directions from a minor. Many misldars were to strike out on their own.

The sun was beginning to set on the powerful Bhangi misl; each successive leader accelerating the nadir of the misl fortunes.

---

[154] A History of the Sikh People by Dr. Gopal Singh p.428 – p.430; While both Latif and Gopal Singh indicate that Charat Singh was a nephew of Ganda Singh, Sohan Singh Seethal depicts him in the Bhangi family tree as Ganda's half-brother.

Desa Singh, leader of the Bhangi misl, and Maha Singh, chief of the Sukerchakia misl, were constantly in the throes of internecine warfare, and Desa Singh killed in a skirmish in 1782. His son, Gulab Singh, was a minor and, therefore, the boy's cousin Karam Singh took over the affairs of the misl as regent.

On attaining adulthood, Gulab Singh, extended his domain around Amritsar where he had made his home. He attacked Kasur, an Afghan stronghold some 75 Km southeast of Amritsar. In 1794, the Afghans fought back and repossessed Kasur. Gulab Singh tried several times to wrest control of Kasur but to no avail.

Gulab Singh was one-dimensional, lacking firmness of character; morally corrupt and indulged in easy vices and was no match to the rival sardars who were busy extending sphere of their control. In 1800, he formed a cabal of Bhangi sardars (Sahib Singh and Gujjar Singh) and Ramgarhia misldar Jassa Singh against Ranjit Singh. Their allied forces faced Ranjit Singh at Bhasin, 15 Km northeast of Lahore. While encamped, Gulab Singh indulged in binge drinking and died.

His son Gurdit Singh succeeded Gulab Singh. As he was a minor, his widowed mother, Musammat Sukhan, conducted the affairs of the misl. At the time, Amritsar was the last and only stronghold of Bhangis. Amritsar, the spiritual center of Sikhism, was also one jewel not in the crown of Ranjit Singh that he hankered after. He needed an excuse to dislodge the

Bhangis, which was to demand the zamzama gun knowing that Sukhan will not yield to his request.[155]

In 1804, with the support of Fateh Singh, sardar of Ahluwalia misl, Sukerchakia chief Ranjit Singh attacked the Bhangi fort and after a few hours prevailed over Gurdit Singh who was awarded a jagir (feudal land grant) in his native village of Panjwar.[156] The once powerful and major branch of the Bhangi misl that reached its zenith under Jhanda Singh and Ganda Singh did thus meet its end.

Gujjar Singh, who led second of the three branches of the Bhangi misl, had three sons (Sukha, Sahib, and Fateh). The brothers quarreled and fought among themselves. Sukha died by fratricide at the hands of Sahib Singh, which made the aging patriarch so despondent that he bequeathed Fateh his estate. An incensed Sahib Singh with the help of his brother-in-law Maha Singh, the then chief of Sukerchakia misl, dispossessed Fateh Singh.

---

[155] History of the Punjab by Syed Muhammad Latif published 1891- p.303
[156] Nearly a dozen families divided Amritsar between them. These families had built fortresses in their localities and maintained retinues of armed tax collectors who mulcted the traders and shopkeepers as often as they could. The leading citizens approached Ranjit Singh (who needed little persuasion) to take over the city. The only family of importance that was likely to put up resistance was that of the widow of the Bhangi sardar (Gulab Singh) who had drunk himself to death at Bhasin three years earlier. The widow occupied the fort of Gobindgarh - A History of the Sikhs by Dr. Gopal Singh.

The family had broken asunder, distressing Gujjar Singh. He mourned the death of his son Sukha and at the same time outraged by Sahib Singh's audacity to strip his brother Fateh of all his estates. Gujjar Singh gathered a large army, forded Chinab River, and set up a blockade of Gujrat. Sahib Singh put up token resistance. He capitulated, sought clemency and forgiven.

The date Gujjar Singh died remains disputed.[157] His death caused Fateh Singh lay claim to his rightful inheritance that his brother Sahib Singh had appropriated, which induced conscience-stricken Maha Singh to champion Fateh Singh's title to his lost estates. The relations between Sahib Singh and Maha Singh curdled. The bad blood between the two erupted in open hostilities in 1792 that pressed Maha Singh to besiege Sodhra fort, in Wazirabad tehsil (administrative division), where Sahib Singh was sheltered. As luck would have it, Maha Singh fell ill and his army walked out on the siege and retreated in disorder to Gujranwala. Three days later Maha Singh died.

Sahib Singh was one of three rulers of Lahore but chose to live in Gujrat, his headquarters. Among the other two were Chet Singh, son of Bhangi sardar Lehna Singh and Mohar Singh, son of Kanhaya sardar Sobha Singh (Sobha Singh was a nephew of the

---

[157] Whereas Syed Muhammad Latif gives the year 1788 of Gujjar Singh's death in Lahore (p.304), Sohan Singh Seethal attests his death to the year 1791(p.27).

illustrious Kanhaya misl chief, Jai Singh). The relationship between these two sardars was fraught with ill will and conflict.

Once a man of vigor and toughness, Sahib Singh's grip on the misl weakened and vitiated because of sapped energy and vitality. Eventually he "became an indolent debauchee and drunkard. He quarreled with rival chiefs and sardars, and, his power thus weakened, Ranjit Singh seized upon all his possessions, which were merged in the new Kingdom which he was now forming".[158] In 1810 Ranjit Singh eventually, at the behest of Sahib Singh's mother, reward him with a valuable jagir (estate), where he passed away the following year.

Lehna Singh who had led the modest third branch of Bhangi misl died in 1797. His son Chet Singh, who was a shadow of his father, succeeded him. Chet Singh upset Muslim subjects of Lahore sector under his control by taking into custody the son of Mian Badar-ud-Din. He was rude and disrespectful towards the Muslim delegation who sought to intervene in the dispute. The unhappy Muslim citizenry implored Ranjit Singh to oust Chet Singh.[159]

---

[158] History of the Punjab by Syed Muhammad Latif published 1891- p.306

[159] According to Sohan Lal, Ranjit Singh's official biographer "The people of Lahore being extremely oppressed, raised their voices of wailing to the skies". The leading citizens sent a secret invitation to Ranjit Singh to come and take the city - A History of the Sikhs by Khushwant Singh – Vol. 1 p.196

The walled city of Lahore had several entrance gates. The three Bhangi sardars occupying Lahore had bricked up all the gates except for the Lahori, Delhi, and Roshmai gates. In 1799, Ranjit Singh and Sada Kaur marched to Lahore with tactical plans of launching a simultaneous assault on Lahori gate by Ranjit Singh and on the Delhi gate by Sada Kaur. Chet Singh had set up his defenses around Lahori gate, as he expected an attack thereon. However, the gate guards informed Chet Singh, falsely, that the Delhi gate was under fire. He was scrambling towards Delhi when the guards at the two gates flung open their doors allowing Sukerchakia sardar free passage to the city. Outmaneuvered, Chet Singh took refuge in Shahi qila (Lahore fort). Sada Kaur was to bring about an agreement between the feuding sardars that would allow Chet Singh a face-saver. Chet Singh would relinquish his suzerainty in return for a profitable jagir. He died in 1815 and his estate reverted to the Sukerchakia sardar.

Mohar Singh, the third of the triumvirate rulers of Lahore, quickly exited the city.[160] His whereabouts are unknown. Since he was a Kanhaya sardar and Sada Kaur was at the time leader of the Kanhaya misl, he may have simply rejoined the family business.

Ranjit Singh's capture of Lahore not just embittered the Bhangi's but also piqued other misldars. It also

---

[160] Mohar Singh was son of Sobha Singh, and latter was a nephew of Jai Singh, the indomitable and larger than life leader of Kanhaya misl

filled Nizamuddin, ruler of prosperous Kasur, with consternation that he would be next in the crosshairs of Ranjit Singh. Therefore, he readily aligned himself with Gulab Singh Bhangi and Jassa Singh Ramgarhia and their allied armies marched towards Lahore and confronted by Ranjit Singh at the village of Bhasin, about 15 Km east of the capital. The two "armies faced each other for two months until the leader of the confederate army, Gulab Singh, died of ill effects of liquor; the others quietly returned to their homes".[161]

The sequential inheritors of the Bhangi misl - once the largest and most powerful misl - precipitated the disintegration of their misl. Each successive overlord if not attempting to seize sole control of the misl was riddled with weakness or imbecility or given to debauch; circumstances that made it simpler for Sukerchakia chieftain Ranjit Singh to hasten eventual death knell of Bhangi sardars.

---

[161] A History of the Sikhs by Khushwant Singh – Vol. 1 p.197-198

Kanhaya Misl

The Kanhaya misl was founded by Jai Singh, a Sandhu Jat of Kahna, a village situated some 10 Km southeast of Lahore and from whence the misl derived its name. Following his baptismal by Kapur Singh, Jai Singh joined the robber band headed by Amar Singh of Khana Kaccha. Jhanda Singh and Singha were his sibling cohorts. Their predatory derring-do made them famous. After pillaging Kasur in 1763 and carrying away substantial booty Jai Singh took up the reins of the misl.[162]

Kanhaya belonged to the Taruna Dal. On Baisakhi day 1748 when Sarbat Khalsa merged the sixty-five independent Jathas into eleven misls under the Dal Khalsa banner, Kanhaya misl was one among them. They were heavily concentrated north of Amritsar in the districts of Batala, Gurdaspur, and Shakargarh between Ravi and Beas Rivers (Bari Doab) with some villages located between Chenab and Ravi Rivers (Rachna Doab).

Quarrels often flared up between misldars over sharing of revenues from disputed properties, particularly when both parties claimed ownership. The ownership of intermingled towns and villages was a serious source of contention; and, the dispute usually resolved by agreement between the misldars on sharing the revenue. Such was not the case

---

[162] History of the Punjab by Syed Muhammad Latif published 1891 p.309

between Jai Singh Kanhaya and Jassa Singh Ramgarhia who locked horns over their possessions straddling River Beas. Kanhaya sardar enlisted the help of Ahluwalia sardar, and in an allied attack expelled the Ramgarhia forces from Srigobindpur. They continued to pursue Jassa Singh Ramgarhia, relentlessly, until uprooted from Bist Doab and relocated to Hissar.

Jai Singh Kanhaya served as a mentor to the young Maha Singh, scion of the chieftain of Sukerchakia misl, Charat Singh; a catalyst sparking youthful sardar's interest in studying conflict among competing interests and understanding of circumstances that prompt individuals and groups to struggle with one another to achieve their different goals.

Jai Singh was instrumental in helping the youngster in his bid to capture Rassulnagar. That triumph imbued Maha Singh with sufficient boldness and self-assurance to make him become master of his own destiny. Thus, reassured Maha Singh set out to plunder Jammu, gathering a large booty and increasing his sphere of control over the neighboring mountain areas. Jai Singh Kanhaya as was custom demanded a share of the spoils and the young Maha Singh ignored his patron's overture. The relations between the two soured.

Anticipating Jai Singh's wrath Maha Singh sought the help of Jassa Singh Ramgarhia, headquartered in Hissar, and other local leaders who had suffered indignities at the hand of the Kanhaya misldar. Chief among them was Gholam Ghous who had lost his hold on Batala to Jai Singh.

In 1784, Sukerchakia and Ramgarhia misls arrayed their troops for battle with the Kanhaya misldar near Achal, about eight miles from Batala. In the ensuing battle Gurbaksh Singh, the older son of Jai Singh, died from an arrow fired into his breast and the sight of their dead leader was the cue for the disheartened followers to flee the battlefield. At the sight of his fallen son, Jai Singh "burst into tears, emptied his quiver of its arrows, and, dismounting from his horse, exposed himself to the enemy's fire. Such was the respect for the old veteran that none dared approach him in his grief, and all quietly withdrew".[163]

Brokenhearted Jai Singh Kanhaya fled to Pathankot. The double whammy of ignominious defeat and the loss of his heir Gurbaksh Singh was the beginning of the decline of the Kanhaya band. Still, Jai Singh was full of vengeance. He gathered whatever forces he could muster and attacked Maha Singh at Naushera. He suffered a severe defeat and retreated to Nurpur, a few kilometers south-west of Anandpur Sahib. Gurbaksh Singh's death "led to the dissolution of the (Kanhaya) misl".[164]

Jai Singh died in 1798. His two sons, Nidhan Singh and Bhag Singh, were inept and not cut out for

---

[163] History of the Punjab by Syed Muhammad Latif published 1891 – p.310 to 311
[164] The Sikh Misls & the Panjab State by Sohan Singh Seetal p.44

leading the once great misl. Their sister-in-law Sada Kaur, widow of Gurbaksh Singh, held with deep affection by Jai Singh, became de facto head of Kanhaya misl. Sada Kaur was shrewd and resourceful. She cleverly maneuvered to get her daughter Mahtab Kaur betrothed to Maha Singh's son and heir Ranjit Singh, whereby she hoped to cement the bonds between the Sukerchakia and Kanhaya misls; and, in 1786 the marriage celebrated with all the traditional pomp and ceremony.

Ranjit Singh was beholden to the Kanhaya misl, which under the chieftainship of Sada Kaur paved his way to capture Lahore and Amritsar. Ranjit Singh valued her support. Sada Kaur had set her sights "to exercise a commanding influence in the affairs of the Sikhs".[165]

When Ranjit Singh set off on his Cis-Sutlej campaign of 1807 his wife, Mahtab Kaur, was pregnant. On his return, he found he had fathered twin boys, Sher Singh and Tara Singh. Rumour swirled in the corridors of the court that Mehtab Kaur had delivered a daughter and that lowly individuals sired the boys. A constant torrent of innuendos revealed, "Sher Singh was the son of a chintz weaver, named Nihala, native of Mokerian, then in the jagir estates of Mai Sada Kaur (and) Tara Singh was the son of a Mohammedan woman, daughter of Manki, a slave girl of Mai Sada Kaur".[166]

---

[165] History of the Sikhs by J.D. Cunningham – p158
[166] The Panjab Chiefs by Sir Lepel H. Griffin p.8

Sada Kaur raised the boys "as if their parentage had been admitted (and) in 1820 Sher Singh was virtually adopted by the Maharaja, with the apparent object of finally setting aside the power of his mother-in-law".[167]

Sada Kaur was not purblind to see that Kharak Singh, born 1802, the first-born son of Ranjit Singh, was next in line for the succession to the Sukerchakia throne.[168] She recognized that her grandsons were a notch below the pecking order. Nonetheless, she continued to nurse an aspiration of elevating Sher Singh in the line for succession.

In 1816, Ranjit Singh formally made Kharak Singh his successor. Sada Kaur was so enraged that she connived with the British against Ranjit Singh whom she accused of dispossessing her. Her conspiratorial role unmade her. Imprisoned for betrayal she died in 1832. On the death of Sada Kaur Ranjit Singh seized all of the Kanhaya possessions. Soon afterwards, Nidhan Singh and Bhag Singh died childless and Ranjit Singh usurped their estates.

However, remnants of Kanhaya misl continued to survive under the important Kanhaya misldari of the

---

[167] ibid
[168] Ranjit Singh was married to the daughter of Nakkai sardar Khazan Singh who bore him Kharak Singh (Cunningham p.158). However, Sohan Singh Seetal indicates that Nakkai sardar Gyan Singh "arranged the marriage of his sister, Raj Kaur, to Maharaja Ranjeet Singh, and she became the mother of Kharak Singh" (The Sikh Misls and the Panjab – p.49)

triumvirate of three brothers Haqiqat Singh, Mehtab Singh, and Sada Singh of village Julka. Haqiqat Singh died in 1782 and his son Jaimal Singh took over the feudal domain. His daughter, Chand Kaur, married Kharak Singh in 1812 and bore him a son named Prince Naunihal Singh. Six months after the wedding Jaimal Singh died and Ranjit Singh confiscated all of his possessions.

Kharak Singh ascended the Lahore throne in 1839 on the death of Ranjit Singh. Following machinations by Dogra family Naunihal Singh usurped the throne and his father Kharak Singh placed in captivity. Maharaja Kharak Singh died in November 1841 and succeeded by Sher Singh who was "assassinated by sirdar Ajit Singh Sindhanwalia on 15th of September 1863".[169]

Thus did the great Kanhaya misl ceased to survive.

---

[169] The Panjab Chiefs by Sir Lepel H. Griffin p.9

Ramgarhia Misl

Unlike other misls, Ramgarhia misl was a renamed misl. Khushal Singh, a Jat, who took his baptism from Banda Bahadur and fought alongside him, was "a notorious robber and commander of an armed force".[170] On his passing, the leadership of the militia devolved upon Nand Singh, a Jat from the village of Sanghana. He styled the group Sanghanian misl and appointed Jassa Singh as its commander.

Jassa Singh assumed the leadership of the misl on the death of Nand Singh. Jassa Singh was the grandson of Hardas Singh, a carpenter from village Sur Singh. Guru Gobind Singh had baptized Hardas Singh. It was his renown for buttressing the fort at Ramgarh from whence the misl renamed itself as the Ramgarhia misl.[171]

The Sikh panth declared Jassa Singh persona non grata on learning that his wife had committed infanticide of her newborn daughter in 1748. Jassa Singh was rankled by the ostracism. An opportunity to vent his rage fell in his lap later in the year at a time when Sikhs were gathering in Amritsar for Diwali celebrations.

---

[170] History of the Punjab by Syed Muhammad Latif published 1891- p.306
[171] The Sikh Misls & the Panjab State by Sohan Singh Seetal p.32- p.33

Apprehensive of the growing power of Sikh misldars in three of the doabs, Mir Mannu, Mughul governor of Punjab, instructed Adina Beg, commander of Jullundur doab, to curb the Sikh leaders. Adina Beg persuaded Jassa Singh Ramgarhia to join his ranks to mount an attack on Amritsar.

When the Mugul and Ramgarhia forces approached the town, hundreds of Sikhs took shelter in the mud-fortress of Ram Rauni, whereupon the fort besieged. With the siege in the second month, the trapped Sikhs ran out of provisions and a number of them starved to death. Realizing a crisis the Sikhs chose one among them to go out disguised as a Mughul to see the lay of the land.

The disguised Sikh scout spotted Jassa Singh among the enemy and berated him for being "the murderer of the Sikhs inside the Ram Rauni". Filled with remorse, Jassa Singh and his men slipped into the fort with supplies in the thick of night. The reinvigorated men reinforced by the Ramgarhia brigade fought valiantly for several days. The high death toll from the assault persuaded Jassa Singh to appeal to Kaura Mal, a Hindu, Diwan of Multan (revenue minister), who was part of the Mogul forces, to spare the Sikh lives.

At that moment, fortuitous circumstances – Ahmad Shah Abdali's second invasion - led to the lifting of the siege as the Moguls diverted their forces to battle the invader, thereby staving off the bad situation faced by the Sikhs. [172]

The timely conversion resulted in forgiveness of Jassa Singh by the Panth. Jassa Singh stayed at the mud fort, rebuilt it with bricks and mortar transforming the fort into a pakka (bricked) fort that came to be known Ramgarh fort; and, the origin of the name Ramgarhia conferred to Jassa Singh.

At their optimum, the Ramgarhia misl had sway over territories between Ravi and Sutlej Rivers. They occupied strongholds of Batala, Kalanaur and Qadian north of Amritsar between Ravi and Beas Rivers; a big chunk of Jullundur Doab comprising Umar Tanda, Megowal, Jullundar and Mukandpur. Jassa Singh allotted Batala to his brother Mali Singh and Kalanaur to his brother Tara Singh. They could muster up an army of ten thousand.

For much of the time Jassa Singh Ramgarhia had a running feud with two other misldars, Jai Singh of the Kanhayias and his namesake Jassa Singh, chief of Ahluwalia misl.

The root of the quarrel with the Kanhaya misl, according to historian Latif, was over "division of revenues of some lands". Jai Singh of Kanhaya misl deputed his gifted son Gurbaksh Singh to attack the Ramgarhia citadel of Batala, then under the charge of

---

[172] The Sikh Misls & the Panjab State by Sohan Singh Seetal – p.33-35

Mali Singh, to exact what was due to them. Mali Singh fled and Batala fell under the control of Kanhayias. Not content with this victory Gurbaksh Singh then marched into the other Ramgarhia stronghold of Kalanaur and expelled Tara Singh. Thus, the Kanhayias wrested control of all Ramgarhia possessions of Bari Doab (between Ravi and Beas Rivers).

Undaunted, Jassa Singh Ramgarhia did recover Batala but was unable to repossess Kalanaur. The feud between the two misls intensified and thousands of their followers died on the battlefield. Each raided other's territory stealing livestock. Eventually Jai Singh overpowered Jassa Singh and drove him beyond the Sutlej River. Amar Singh, chief of the Phoolkian misl, gave succor to Jassa Singh during his flight, helping him relocate to Hissar region, where the Ramgarhias "lived on the gains of plunder".[173]

The next encounter between Jassa Singh Ramgarhia and Jai Singh Kanhayia took place in 1784. This came about because of a quarrel that the youthful Sukerchkia sardar Maha Singh had picked up with Jai Singh by refusing to share the spoils of Jammu. Maha Singh sent an emissary to Hissar with the appeal to Jassa Singh to join him to resist an impending attack from Jai Singh (see Kanhaya misl section for details of the battle). Suffice it to say the battle marked the eclipse of the Kanhaya misl.

---

[173] The Sikh Misls & the Panjab State by Sohan Singh Seetal – p.38

Both the chieftains of Ramgarhia misl and Ahluwalia misl shared the same name Jassa Singh. Their relations turned sour when they first faced one another at the battle of Dina Nagar (circa 1774). They were not the primary antagonists because the battle was a settling of scores between Ganda Singh, chief of Bhangi misl and Jai Singh Kanhaya. Ganda Singh sought to punish the Kanhayias for their complicity in the killing of his brother Jhanda Singh and for refusing the return of the estate of Pathankot (see Bhangi section for details of the incident). In this battle, Ramgarhia formed alliance with the Bhangis while Ahluwalias backed the Kanhayias.

Ahluwalia sardar was somewhat irked by the role played by the Ramgarhia sardar. Relations worsened when Mali Singh, brother of Jassa Singh Ramgarhia, accosted Jassa Singh Ahluwalia while on a hunt with his companions near the Nangal village (circa 1776). The encounter resulted in a pitched fight. Taken into custody, a wounded Jassa Singh Ahluwalia was "carried in a palanquin" to Srigobindpur, the capital town of Ramgarhias.[174] The account of the encounter by Sohan Singh Seetal is at odds with that of Gopal Singh.[175]

The whole episode was a great embarrassment for the Ramgarhia chief who felt it was no way "to avenge

---

[174] A History of the Sikh People by Dr. Gopal Singh p.429
[175] The Sikh Misls & the Panjab State by Sohan Singh Seetal at page 37 sets a scene indicating Ahluwalia chief "went to Acchal for a holy bath in 1776 (and) was attacked by Tara Singh, Mali Singh and Khushal Singh".

one's wrongs in this surreptitious way". The Ramgarhia chief made an apology, showered gifts on the Ahluwalia chief, and "escorted him out of his territory".[176]

Nonetheless, the Ahluwalia chief left in a fit of pique. A chance to obtain retribution against the Ramgarhia chief came his way as Jai Singh, the Kanhaya chief, and Jassa Singh Ramgarhia, locked horns over the sharing of revenues of "some possessions which were claimed by both parties, their territories in upper Bari Doab and upper Jullundur Doabs intermingling with each other's". Jassa Singh Ahluwalia allied himself with the Kanhaya misl. Even after ousting the Ramgarhia garrison from Srigobindpur, the Kanhaya-Ahluwalia alliance, determined totally to obliterate Ramgarhia presence from the Doabs, continued their march and expelled them from their strongholds of Batala and Kalanaur. Tara Singh, the brother of Jassa Singh Ramgarhia, died in the attack; and, the other brother, Khushal Singh, seriously wounded. The Ramgarhias fled to Hissar "which became their home for sometime thereafter".[177]

However, that was not to be the end of Ramgarhia-Ahluwalia vendetta. The two misldars got embroiled in the conflict between Jai Singh, chief of Kanhaya misl and Maha Singh, chief of Sukerchakia misl. The cause of disagreement was the refusal by Maha Singh

---

[176] A History of the Sikh People by Dr. Gopal Singh p.429
[177] ibid – p.429 - 430

to share the spoils of the loot in Jammu with the Kanhaya chief as per protocol (circa 1782).

Maha Singh lured the Ramgarhia chief, now established in Hissar, to join forces with him against the Kanhaya misl and the quid pro quo was the recovery by the Ramgarhias of their lost territories in Bari Doab. In a preemptive strike, Maha Singh launched an assault on the Kanhayian headquarters at Batala (see Kanhaya misl section for details of the battle). Sukerchakia-Ramgarhia forces prevailed and Jassa Singh Ramgarhia succeeded in re-occupying Batala.

The re-capture of Batala by Jassa Singh Ramgarhia from their grip greatly agitated Kanhayias, now under the leadership of Sada Kaur. Whether because he felt the Kanhayias were a spent force or that a woman headed the misl, Jassa Singh Ramgarhia continued to attack and harass the Kanhayias. Threatened and fazed Sada Kaur appealed to Ranjit Singh, now chief of Sukerchakia misl, to help her fend off the Ramgarhia assaults.

In 1796, the combined forces of Sukerchakia-Kanhaya misls lay siege to the fort at Maini on the banks of Beas River occupied by Jassa Singh but had to abandon the siege because of the flooded river. At the end of the year, Ranjit Singh attacked Batala and routed the Ramgarhias, an event that finally crippled the Ramgarhia misl and bringing down the curtain on their dominance of the Doabs.[178]

The year Jassa Singh Ramgarhia died is in dispute. Seetal claims that he died in 1803.[179] According to Cunningham, in 1807 "the place (Kasur) was invested by Ranjit Singh, and by Jodh Singh Ramgarhia, the son of his father's old ally, Jassa the Carpenter"[180]. From this, one can figure out that Jassa Singh had died prior to Jodh Singh taking over the reins of the Ramgrhia misl, and that has to be before 1807.

Jassa Singh died leaving behind two sons Jodh Singh and Bir Singh, the former succeeding as the leader of the misl. Jodh Singh joined the retinue of Ranjit Singh. His demise in 1815 set off a quarrel among his successors that prompted Ranjit Singh to appropriate all of the Ramgarhia territories and in return award a

---

[178] The Sikh Misls & the Panjab State by Sohan Singh Seetal p.38
[179] The Sikh Misls & the Panjab State by Sohan Singh Seetal p.38; ibid. – p.38; Syed Muhmmad Latif, on the other hand, provides an altogether different narrative. Firstly, he gives 1816 as the year of the demise of Jassa Singh. Secondly, he goes on to say : "Jodh Singh died, leaving a son, Hira Singh, but all the possessions of the misl were now seized by Ranjit Singh, son of Maha Singh, who, on his return from Kangra, in 1808, imprisoned Bir Singh, Dewan Singh and Hira Singh". From this, it is reasonable to infer that when Ranjit Singh seized Ramgarhia misl territories in 1808 that Jassa Singh was already dead. Considering the credentials of Latif it is likely there is a typographical error: he may have meant the year 1806 and not 1816 as printed (History of the Punjab by Syed Muhammad Latif published 1891– p.308-309)
[180] History of the Sikhs by J.D. Cunningham p.121

pension to most of the members of the extended family.[181]

Seetal's aforementioned version of how the Ramgarhia misl met its end is at odds with that of Latif. According to Latif Ranjit Singh "went to Amritsar, and laid siege to the fort of Ram Rouni, which he took. The Maharaja took city after city, and razed to the ground the strongholds of the Ramgarhias to the number of a hundred and fifty, all within a very short time (and) the remnants of the once powerful Ramgarhia misl, which, like other misls, collapsed and fell before the all-absorbing power of the future Maharaja of the Panjab".[182]

---

[181] The Sikh Misls & the Panjab State by Sohan Singh Seetal p.39
[182] History of the Punjab by Syed Muhammad Latif published 1891– p.309

Singhpuria Misl

Kapur Singh founded the Singhpuria misl, sometimes referred to as Fyzulpuria misl.[183] He was born in the village of Kaloke situated just west of the Chenab River, and belonged to the Virk clan. He was among the person gathered in Amritsar on Diwali day who was administered amrit (baptism) by Bhai Mani Singh.

Kapur Singh was the most distinguished and respected Sikh of his times. He is reputed to have persuaded myriads of people from all occupations and social class and clans to embrace Sikhism and administered baptism to many of them. Circa 1735, he baptized Ala Singh, sardar of Phulkian misl, and several other members of the family.

Following Banda Bahadur's execution, the Mogul emperor tasked Zakariya Khan, governor of Lahore, to hound and hunt down the Sikhs. Kapur Singh conscripted men at peril to form a band to resist the Mogul repression, a band that later came to be known as Singhpuria misl. At the peak, Kapur Singh commanded an army of well-trained 2,500 soldiers renowned for their fierce fighting spirit. Though a small misl, they were the most dreaded band.

---

[183] Kapur Singh had wrested the village of Fyzullpurra, near Amritsar, from its Mahomedan founder. He had also captured several surrounding villages, one of which was renamed Singhpuria – Latif p.322

The misl built headquarters in a remote hill fastness. As word would reach them of Mogul revenue collectors in the vicinity, they would descend on the plains to hijack the treasury. These heists so frustrated the Mogul government that they decided to hold out to an olive branch to the Sikhs.[184]

There is no mention in any chronicle indicating that Singhpuria misl was engaged in banditry, as did other misls.

As leader of the Panth (Sikh collectivity), Kapur Singh had tremendous support. Following his appointment as commander of the Budha Dal on Baisakhi day 1733, and later as recognized commander of Singhpuria misl, one of the eleven misls incorporated into Dal Khalsa, he enjoyed immense prestige.

Kapur Singh was not just the godfather of Jassa Singh Ahluwalia, he, also baptized him. When he died in 1753, as per his wish, the leadership of the Panth

---

[184] The Sikh Misls & the Panjab State by Sohan Singh Seetal p.50-51; Bahadur Zakaria Khan, Governor of Lahore, sent his emissary Shabeg Singh to the congregation of Sikhs assembled in Amritsar on Baisakhi celebrations held in 1733, with title deeds of a nawabship (a Mahomedan title of a ruling prince or powerful landowner)and a grant of largess. The congregants unanimously named Kapur Singh as the recipient of the title. Diwan Darbara Singh headed the Sikh Panth (Sikh collectivity) and when he died in July 1734 Nawab Kapur Singh became the leader of the Panth.

passed to Jassa Singh.[185] He died childless in 1753 and his nephew Khushal Singh inherited the leadership of the Singhpuria misl. Two years later Budh Singh took over the reins in 1795.[186]

In 1811, Budh Singh flouted a summons from Ranjit Singh. Latter was so outraged that he ordered his general Mokham Chand and Fateh Singh, chieftain of Ahluwalia misl, to divest Budh Singh of all his possessions. Budh Singh vacated his Ludhiana headquarters and went over to the British seeking asylum.

---

[185] A History of the Sikh People by Dr. Gopal Singh – footnote at p.366

[186] Guru Arjun Dev had arranged for laying a flight of steps leading down the tank at Tarn Taran. Nur Din, a Muslim headman, appropriated the bricks and used them to build his house in his village of Sarai Nurdin, 7 km northwest of Tarn Taran. Guru Arjun Dev prophesied that those bricks would one day furbish the tank. Budh Singh, chieftain of Singhpuria misl, was to fulfill that prophesy by dismantling Nur Din's house and carrying the bricks to Tar Taran to complete the steps.

Karorasinghian Misl

A triumvirate of whom the prominent leader, Karori Mal, a Jat of village Panjgarh, took the name Karora Singh on taking amrit (baptism) founded the misl. Mastan Singh and Karam Singh were the other two companions.[187] The misl bore one of two names: one associated with the name of the leader (Karorasinghian) and the other linked to his village (Panjgharia).

Seetal on the other hand claims that Sham Singh of Village Naarli founded the misl, and that when killed in action against Nadir Shah in 1739, Karam Singh, his comrade-in-arms, became the leader. Karora Singh became the next leader of the band when Karam Singh died in action in 1746.[188]

Ganda Singh and Seetal differ greatly on who killed Diwan Bishamber Dass, Diwan of Doaba, in a battle fought near Urmar Tanda, situated 40 Km north of Jalandhar. Ganda Singh depicts Jassa Singh Ahulwalia, sword in hand, leading an attack against the Diwan.

---

[187] History of the Punjab by Syed Muhammad Latif published 1891 – p.323.

[188] The Sikh Misls & the Panjab State by Sohan Singh Seetal – p65 p.65 another version has Karorha Singh (sic) form a separate jatha of his own in 1748, named after him and he became a Jathedar of Taruna Dal. Brief History of Sikh Misls published by Sikh Missionary College (Regd,), Ludhiana – Publication No. 360

One of arrows showered by Jassa Singh killed Bishamber Dass.[189] Seetal credits Karora Singh to have "beheaded Diwan Bishambhar Das".[190]

Late in 1763 proxies for Jawahar Singh, King of Bharatpur, appealed to Jassa Singh Ahluwalia to help curb the Rohilla tribal chief Nijab-ul- Daula, governor of Saharanpur, who was terrorizing his kingdom Saharanpur.[191] Desiring to decimate Afghan influence and at same time spread Khalsa dominance in the region, Jassa Singh, in February 1764, mobilized an army of 40,000 horse cavalry, under the command of several prominent misldars that included Karora Singh, and mounted an attack against Nijab-ul- Daula.

Karora Singh died in battle and being childless his associate Baghel Singh, a Dhaliwal Jat, who was one of many sardars in the campaign of Saharanpur against Nijab-ul- Daula, took over the reins of the Karorasinghian misl. Recognized as most formidable of the Sikh leaders, Bagel Singh vastly extended the

---

[189] Sardar Jassa Singh Ahluwalia by Ganda Singh – p. 99
[190] The Sikh Misls & the Panjab State by Sohan Singh Seetal p.65
[191] Dal Khalsa army broke their camp near Buriya (now in Haryana), on February 20, 1764 crossed Jamuna River and captured the city. They then rampaged through Nijab-ul-Daula's domain that included Shamli, Deoband, Muzaffarnagar, Jwalapur and Najibabad (the city founded by him); towns lying on an arc stretching from south-west to south-east in distances varying between 30 km to 90 km from Saharanpur. Nijab-ul-Daula sued for peace by offering to pay an annual tribute to the Dal Khalsa. For detail, refer to Sardar Jassa Singh Ahluwalia by Ganda Singh – p.136-137

area of his influence to east of Sutlej and exercised much control in Jalandhar Doaba. He is reputed to control 12,000 fighting men.

In 1769 Baghel Singh, Karorasinghian misldar, was outraged that Amar Singh, chief of Phulkian misl, had usurped some of his villages that included Lalru and Bhunni near Ambala and village of Mullanpur situated 20 Km west of Ludhiana. The two adversaries faced each other near Ghurram, some 20 Km south of Patiala. Amar Singh negotiated a truce.

In the decade from 1773 to 1783 Baghel Singh in consort with Tara Singh Gheba, sardar of Dallewalian misl and Rai Singh, a prominent Bhangi misldar, swept through a vast swath of territory between Jamna River and Ganges River, looting cities and towns that included Gangoh, Ambehta, Nanauta, Deoband, Amir Nagar, Kas Ganj and suburbs of Delhi. These forays so unhinged the Mogul emperor Shah Alam ll that he sent his emissary to negotiate a treaty with the Sikhs allowing latter to maintain their sphere of control in the Jamna-Ganges Doab in return for a specified yearly payoff and a promise that Sikhs would cease plundering that territory.

Baghel Singh stayed encamped in Sabzi Mandi suburb of Delhi with a force of 4,000 horsemen while the rest of the allied misl forces returned to Punjab. It was during this sojourn that Baghel Singh built the

Bangla Sahib, Sis Ganj and Rakab Ganj gurdwaras.[192] After a while, Baghel returned to Punjab.

Mogul emperor Shah Alam ll was in a limbo in Bihar and his hold on Delhi was tenuous during the period 1761 to 1771. He faced the quartet of East India Company in the east, Marathas trampling across northern India, Sikhs despoiling Trans-Jamna region, and Nijab-ul- Daula firmly ensconced in Delhi as administrator.[193]

The disarray in Delhi prompted Baghel Singh and Jassa Singh Ramgarhia to irrupt into the trans-Jamna region to pillage Chandausi. On seeing approaching East India Company forces the Sikhs withdrew across Jamna. In 1785, the Marathas who were de facto

---

[192] The Sikh Misls & the Panjab State by Sohan Singh Seetal p.68-70

[193] In 1764 the emperor Shah Alam ll and Shuja-ud-Daula, Nawab of Oudh, threatened by expanding influence of the English led a joint expedition against them and were defeated at the battle of Baksar. In return for conferring Diwani of Bengal, Bihar and Orissa on the East India Company, the English lodged Shah Alam in Allahabad. Meanwhile Maratha made their presence felt in northern India after approached by the emperor to help him wrest control of Delhi. Shah Alam "remained a helpless puppet in the hands of his ministers and the Marathas". Shah Alam's expedition to Rajasthan (circa 1784) so entangled him that Ghulam Qadir Ruhela, grandson of Nijab-ul- Daula, deposed him in 1788. Once again, the emperor appealed to Mahadji Sindhia who recovered Delhi. Court intrigues continued and in 1803, Lord Lake captured Delhi and pensioned off Shah Alam. – The Mogul Empire by Ashirbadilal Srivastava – p. 436-439

rulers of Delhi entered into a quid pro quo arrangement whereby on payment of a yearly tribute the Sikh misldars would not despoil their domain. Most of Baghel Singh's possessions were located in the Cis-Sutlej region, only some were in the Jullundur Doab. When Bagel Singh died in 1798, Ranjit Singh seized his estate in the Doab and granted his wife a jagir (feudal land ownership).

When Baghel Singh died in 1798, the leadership passed to Jodh Singh, son of Gurbaksh Singh, a prominent sardar of Karorasinghian misl and a close associate of Baghel Singh. Gurbaksh Singh was the founder and ruler of Kalsia state situated about 25 Km northwest of Maler Kotlka.

Jodh Singh was a resourceful and capable leader who conquered Dera Bassi (a town just south of present day Chandigarh) and several other villages. He rendered valuable service to Ranjit Singh at the 1807 siege of Naraingarh and handsomely rewarded with jagirs.[194] On his demise in 1818, Karorasinghian misl was absorbed into the Kalsia family and under the command of his son Sobha Singh.

Sobha Singh was beholden to the British who sheltered his possessions in the Cis-Sutlej region. He also provided critical help to the British during the 1857 mutiny.

---

[194] History of the Punjab by Syed Muhammad Latif published 1891 – p.324

Dallewalian Misl

Dallewalian misl was founded by Gulab Singh in 1748 and was named after his native village of Dhaliwal, situated about 20 Km south of Jullundur. Gulab Singh died in battle in 1755 and succeeded by his relative Gurdial Singh. Tara Singh took over the leadership when Gurdial Singh fell fighting. Tara Singh had earned his nickname Gheba from the manner in which he drove his flock across mountain valleys.

Dallewalian misl owned territories that straddled both sides of Sutlej River with villages and towns spread between Jullundur Doab and Malwa. Most of the time his misl aligned with other Malwa based misls to confront the foe or a rival. He died in 1807 in Rahon, his headquarters.

Ranjit Singh annexed all the territories and awarded jagirs to Tara Singh's sons. The widow had relocated to Ludhiana and became a pensioner of the East India Company.

Nakkai Misl

Hira Singh of Bahrwal village in the province of Multan founded the Nakkai misl. He took control of Nakka country, a region south-west of Lahore and bordering on Multan, between the Rivers Ravi and Sutlej, from whence the misl derived its name of Nakkai.

In 1766, Hira Singh mounted an attack on Pakpattan and killed in action. His son being a minor, his nephew Nahar Singh took over the misl leadership. In 1768 on the death of Nahar, at the battle of Kot Kamalia, a town 80 Km north-west of Pakpattan, leadership passed onto his brother Ran Singh.

Ran Singh was a powerful chieftain. His commanded 2,000 horsemen and was instrumental in extending widely his misl's sphere of control. He died in 1781 and was succeeded by his eldest son Bhagwan Singh

An internecine feud between the prominent Nakkai sardars of the misl, Bhagwan Singh and Wazir Singh erupted in Amritsar in 1785 in which the former killed. His brother Gyan Singh succeeded Bhagwan Singh. Gyan Singh arranged the marriage of his sister, Raj Kaur, to Ranjit Singh Sukerchakia and she gave birth to Kharak Singh.[195]

Gyan Singh died in 1807 and his son Kahn Singh took over the reins of the misl. In 1810, Ranjit Singh appropriated Nakkai misl possessions and granted these to his son Kharak Singh; and, Kahn Singh pensioned off.

---

[195] The Sikh Misls & the Panjab State by Sohan Singh Seetal p.49; however, Latif has a very different account of which brother arranged the marriage. According to Latif, at page 313, "Ran Singh was succeeded by his eldest son, Bhagwan Singh, who married his sister, Musammat Raj Kaur, to Ranjit Singh, son of Maha Singh Sukerchakia"

Shaheedan Misl

Baba Deep Singh of village Pahuwind, near Tarn Taran, founded the Shaheedan misl. He received his baptism from Guru Gobind Singh and fought many a battles alongside the Guru. He was a comrade-in-arms of Banda Bahadur. As he was wont to spearhead most of the battles, his band earned the name Shaheedan (band of martyrs).

Abdali's fourth invasion netted him a great deal of treasure. As he was making his way to Lahore, Sikh bands ambushed and pillaged his train at many places. Abdali was so enraged that he vented his anger by marching into Amritsar and blowing up Harminder Sahib and defiled the sacred pool.

The news of desecration reached Baba Deep Singh who was at the time custodian of Damdama Sahib. The news so tormented him that he gathered his band and headed for Amritsar. Thousands of Sikhs joined the band en route. At the same time, Prince Taimur ordered Afghan General Jahan Khan to intercept the Sikhs. At the battle fought near Goharwal (circa 1757), the Sikhs were no match for the well-armed Afghans; Baba Deep Singh was killed.[196]

---

[196] Deep Singh is one of the most revered heroes of Sikh history. Colour prints show him running with his head on his left palm, still wielding his sword with his right (A History of the Sikhs by Khushwant Singh – Vol. 1 p.146)

Sadda Singh succeeded Baba Deep Singh and when killed in a battle of Dakoha with the Afghans in 1762, leadership passed to Karam Singh. As most of the misl possessions lay east of the Sutlej River in the Malwa region, Karam Singh chose to locate his headquarters to Shahzadpur, a village about 24 Km north-east of Ambala. He donated a dozen freehold villages to Damdama Sahib.

Karam Singh fought many battles under the Dal Khalsa confederacy but he set a shining example in the 1773 assault on Jalalabad.[197] He died in 1784 and his son, Gulab Singh took over the reins of the misl. In 1804, self-interest drove him to seek the protection of the British.

Nishanwalia Misl

Dasaunda Singh of village Mansoor was the standard-bearer of Dal Khalsa. He founded Nishanwalia misl, a name derived from carrying the standard.[198] The misl,

---

[197] A Brahmin of Jalalabad came to Amritsar and appealed to the Panth to rescue his daughter from the clutches of Hassan Khan, ruler of Jalalabad, who had abducted her. Karam Singh took up the cause and with the support of Baghel Singh, chief of Karorasinghian misl, they crossed the Jamuna River sacked Nanauta and in December 1773 killed Hassan Khan and pillaged his city and neighbouring villages. The girl rescued and united with her husband and given a financial award.

[198] The Sikh Misls & the Panjab State by Sohan Singh Seetal - p.60, Khuswant Singh, too, appears to indicate Dasuanda Singh as the founder. However, Latif is at odds with both Seetal and Khushwant Singh. According to Latif, Nishanwalia misl was

headquartered in Ambala, controlled about 12,000 troops. As the misl that carried the standard, they were involved in most of the campaigns of Dal Khalsa.

In February 1764 Jassa Singh Ahluwalia, supreme commander of Dal Khalsa, mobilized an army of 40,000 horse cavalry made up of Dallewalian misl, Kanhaya misl, Bhangi misl, Shaheedan misl and the Nishanwalia misl and marched across Jamna River and mounted an attack against Nijab-ul- Daula, governor of Saharanpur.[199]

Dasaunda Singh died in action and succeeded by his brother Sangat Singh. Sangat Singh chose to relocate to the village of Singhanwala, about 200 Km west of Ambala in the district of Ferozpur. He appointed Gurbaksh Singh as ruler of Ambala. Ten years later (1774), Sangat Singh died and, as his sons were minors, Dhian Singh appointed regent.

When the older sibling, Mehar Singh, came of age, he took control of the misl. He died in battle with the ruler of Murinda, a town about 30 Km north-west of present day Chandigarh. Although Mehar Singh had

---

founded by Sangat Singh and Mohar Singh, the standard bearers of Dal Khalsa, from whence the misl derived its name (History of the Punjab by Syed Muhammad Latif published 1891 – p.322). However, Seetal, in his Nishanwalia family tree shows Sangat Singh to be the brother of Dasaunda Singh and uncle to Mehar Singh (Mohar as spelled by Latif.

[199] for more details about the campaign refer to the sketch on Karorasinghia misl

two younger brothers (Kapur Singh and Anoop Singh), Gurbaksh Singh supplanted himself as de facto ruler of Ambala. On his passing, his widow Daya Kaur took over control of Ambala and although Ranjit Singh wrested it from her in 1808, Ranjit Singh had to cede it to Daya Kaur because of the British taking over governance of Malwa territory.[200]

---

[200] The Sikh Misls & the Panjab State by Sohan Singh Seetal p.61 – Latif, on the other hand, provides a contradictory account. At Page 322, Latif writes: "Mohar Singh died without issue; and Ranjit Singh, who was encamped on the other side of the Sutlej, hearing of his death, deputed his dewan, Mokham Chand, at the head of the army, to reduce the misl. Ranjit's troops soon drove the Nishanwalia from the field, terminating the existence of the misl".

Ahluwalia Misl

Sadhu Singh founded the village of Ahlu from whence the family derives its name of Ahluwalia. His bloodline can be traced to Bhatti Rajputs of Jaisalmer, whose descendants settled in Punjab (Chak Taran Taran) and with "passage of time they got mingled with the Jats", the majority community of the area.[201] Latif claims that Sadhu (Sadao as spelled by Latif) was "a Jat, kalal, or distiller".[202]

Sadhu Singh grew up in his maternal village. His childhood playmates belonged to the kalal (wine merchant) families. A young girl of one of the kalal families captivated him. After he returned to his paternal village of Ahlu, he declared his love for the girl and his desire to marry her. The father of the girl gave his consent on a condition that Sadhu (Sadhawa as spelled by Seetal) adopts the kalal caste and vow henceforth that his progeny will exclusively marry into families of Kalal.[203]

Sadhu's great grandson Badar Singh married the sister of Bhagu, a Kalal. Bhagu was administered baptism by Nawab Kapur Singh, commander of Budhha Dal, whereupon Bhagu changed his name to Bhag Singh. He was a brigand of such note that several other

---

[201] Sardar Jassa Singh Ahluwalia by Ganda Singh – p.3
[202] History of the Punjab by Syed Muhammad Latif published 1891 p.313
[203] The Sikh Misls & the Panjab State by Sohan Singh Seetal – p. 75

desperados became a member of his band and the gang was forerunner of misl Ahluwalia

In 1718, Badar Singh begets a son whom he named Jassa Singh. The boy was five years old when his father died. The storyline dealing with the upbringing of Jassa Singh has different versions. Some of the particulars as told by Syed Muhammad Latif, Ganda Singh, Sohan Singh Seetal, and Gopal Singh differ materially from one another.

On one point, they all agree upon is that Jassa Singh's mother took the boy to Delhi to meet Mata Sundri, widow of Guru Gobind Singh, who blessed the boy and foretold that he would one day achieve greatness.

Latif narrates that the young Jassa Singh and mother lived with Bhag Singh in Jullundur. On a visit to Bhag Singh's home, Nawab Kapur Singh sees and hears young Jassa singing the "ballads in adoration of the Guru" in concert with his mother. He was so impressed with the boy's rendition of holy hymns that he asked the mother that the boy made his ward. Kapur Singh raised Jassa Singh as his own child.[204]

According to Ganda Singh Mata Sundri was so touched by Jassa Singh's "religious bent of mind and his love for Gurbani" that she made mother and child stay with her in Delhi for next seven years during which time Jassa Singh "studied religious and

---

[204] History of the Punjab by Syed Muhammad Latif published 1891 p.314

historical books" and acquired proficiency in Persian, language of Mogul court.. However, maternal Uncle Bhag Singh sought custody of the boy and in 1730 Mata Sundri gave her consent for Bhag Singh to take his sister and nephew, now thirteen years old, to live with him in Jullundur. One gurpurb (religious celebration) day Bagh Singh accompanied by his sister and nephew Jassa Singh met with Nawab Kapur Singh who was so highly impressed with their recitation of Asa-di-Var (selected hymns from the sacred scriptures) that he asked Bhag Singh "to leave the boy with him (and that) from then onwards be his own son". Later, Kapur Singh administered Khande-di-Pahul to Jassa Singh.[205]

Sohan Singh Seetal's version is that "when Jassa Singh was seventeen years old, his uncle, sardar Bhag Singh, took the boy and his mother back to the Punjab from Delhi" and while en route, they stayed with "Nawab Kapur Singh at Kartarpur". Mother and son sang morning hymns (Asa-di-Var) and the musical recital so "mightily pleased" Kapur Singh that he took Jassa "in his lap and declared: you are my adopted son from this day".[206]

Dr. Gopal Singh's rendition is that "Mata Sundri asked Nawab Kapur Singh to take charge of the promising youth. Both he and his mother used to perform the Hari-Kirtan before the Nawab who

---

[205] Sardar Jassa Singh Ahluwalia by Ganda Singh – p.8 – p10
[206] The Sikh Misls & the Panjab State by Sohan Singh Seetal – p. 76

much pleased at his supreme devotion to the faith (that he) appointed him also a storekeeper with his forces".[207]

When Bhag Singh "died without issue, the sardari of the misl devolved on his sister's son, Jassa Singh (whose) political talents, religious zeal and loft aspirations combined, rendered him one of the most powerful federal chiefs of the Panjab". According to Seetal, Jassa Singh relinquished his association with the "band of Nawab Kapur Singh (and) formed his own band, afterwards in 1745".[208]

At a meeting assembled in Amritsar, at the time of Baisakhi, on March 29, 1748, Sarbat Khalsa folded the sixty-five independent Jathas into eleven misls under the umbrella of Dal Khalsa. Jassa Singh Ahluwalia took over the leadership from the aging Kapur Singh and anointed as supreme commander of Dal Khalsa.

There was bad blood between the two namesakes: Jassa Singh, sardar of Ahluwalia misl and Jassa Singh, sardar of Ramgarhia misl. The bitter enemies fought in 1775 at Zahura, Hoshiarpur, in which Ramgarhia chief wounded and he then retreated. The Ahluwalia sardar awarded Zahura to Baghel Singh, chief of the Karorasinghian misl.

---

[207] A History of the Sikh People by Dr. Gopal Singh p.383 (footnote)
[208] The Sikh Misls & the Panjab State by Sohan Singh Seetal – p. 76

In 1776, Ramgarhias had waylaid Jassa Singh Ahluwalia and his hunting party near the village of Nangal, an encounter that left a deep-seated feeling of rancour in the Ahluwalia leader. Not long after an opportunity came his way to settle accounts with the Ramgarhia sardar that ended in the complete ouster of the Ramgarhia misl from Doab area, resulting in their fleeing to the Malwa region of Hissar.[209]

Jassa Singh Ahluwalia was perhaps the only misldar who was literate. Leading sardars held him in such high esteem that they were themselves baptized by him, including Amar Singh chief of the Phulkian misl. His reputation built not so much on miri - the strength of his misl did not exceed 4,000 armed men - as it was on piri, seen as a religious leader, a mantle placed on him following the demise of Nawab Kapur Singh. He was a strict adherent of the tenets of Sikh faith. Unlike other sardars known for their hard drinking, he practiced abstinence.

Jassa Singh died in October 1783 while on the way from Fatehbad to Amritsar to partake in the Diwali celebrations. He was childless and succeeded by his cousin, Bhag Singh. Bhag Singh twice attacked Jassa Singh Ramgarhia. Latter then enlisted the help of Sansar Chand, a scion of the Katoch dynasty that had ruled Kangra for some centuries, to launch an allied attack on the Ahluwalias.

---

[209] Sardar Jassa Singh Ahluwalia by Ganda Singh – p. 198-199

In 1801, Ramgarhia allied forces routed Ahluwalia army under the command of sardar Hamir Singh and the general wounded. Bhag Singh took over command and marched to Phagwara, a city 22 Km southeast of Jullundur, to do battle with the Ramgarhia. He fell ill and taken back to Kapurthala where he died the same year.

Fateh Singh succeeded Bhag Singh and he and Ranjit Singh swore "perpetual friendship on the sacred Granth, and exchanged turbans in token of brotherhood".[210]

The survival of the Ahluwalia misl rested on two elements. Firstly, among the important misls it was the only one that observed strict discipline and cohesiveness and not riven with factional fighting or family usurpers. Secondly, under the aegis of Ranjit Singh the Ahluwalias continued to reign over their territory. The misl made Kapurthala, a city situated 18 Km northeast of Jullundur, as their headquarters and to this day the family continues to go by the name of Ahluwalia.

---

[210] History of the Punjab by Syed Muhammad Latif published 1891 p.317

Phulkian Misl

The ruling families of Patiala, Nabha, Jind, Faridkot, and Ataari are all descended from Raja Rawal Jaisal, a Bhatti Rajput ruler, who founded the city of Jaisalmar circa 1156 in what today is Rajasthan. The fifteenth descendant by name of Baraar had two sons: Paur and Dhaul. Paur is the progenitor of the rulers of Patiala, Nabha, and Jind; and, Dhaul is the ancestor of the rulers of Faridkot.[211]

Phul, a Bhatti Rajput belonging to Siddhu Jat tribe, thirtieth in descent from Raja Jaisal, eleventh in descent from Paur, founded the village of Phul, five miles east of village Mehraj and some forty miles north east of Bhatinda in the state of Nabha. By a Royal edict (ferman), Emperor Shah Jahan appointed him as a Chaudhary (a title conferring ancestral ownership of land).

Phul founded the Phulkian misl. He became a powerful sardar and a dominant force who was oft-times engaged in hostilities with neighbouring Muslim chiefs. The Governor of Jagraon took him into custody for withholding revenues and died in 1652 while a prisoner. His sons (seven by Latif's count; six as indicated by Seetal in his Phulkian family tree) established personal rule in Patiala, Jhind, Nabha and Faridkot and by all accounts remained friendly and always acted in each other's interests.

---

[211] The Sikh Misls & the Panjab State by Sohan Singh Seetal p.91-92

None of the rulers of the aforementioned principalities was, therefore, sons of the soil of Punjab. For starters, their dominions were located outside of Punjab in the Malwa region of Cis-Sutlej. They were outsiders who had not assimilated into the culture of the people they ruled. Moreover, as noted earlier, Phulkian misl was the only misl that was not a member of Dal Khalsa.

It was under Phuls grandson, Ala Singh, a strong-willed man of indomitable spirit, that the misl was to blossom. He rehabilitated the town of Barnala and made it his capital. His domain consisted of over thirty villages.

In 1731 Ala Singh came under attack from Rai Kallha, Rajput chief of Raikot, a town some twenty kilometers south-east of Jagraon. "Jamal Khan, chief of Malerkotla, and Nawab Saiyad Asad Ali Khan, the imperial faujdar of the Jullundur Doab", supported Rai.[212] In a fiercely fought battle faujdar and a large number of enemy troops killed, while others fled the battlefield.

This victory over the Rajputs and Pathans made Ala Singh a powerful force not to be antagonized. His neigbouring rulers were in awe of him and a large number of men flocked to join his band. He extended his realm through conquering of other villages and building new ones. His fame reached the Mogul

---

[212] History of the Punjab by Syed Muhammad Latif published 1891 p.326

emperor, Muhammad Shah, who appointed him as functionary of Sirhind with a chance of becoming its raja.

In 1735, Sardar Kapoor Singh and his military force entered Barnala. Ala Singh arranged recitation of the Granth Sahib and following the path (recitation) he and several family members submitted for baptism. Thus, Ala Singh, a Rajput, embraced the Sikh faith.

The role of Phulkian misl is nothing to speak of in the long protracted campaign by the misls of Dal Khalsa to have complete hegemony over Punjab. The policy of the Phulkian sardars "veered round their immediate advantage. When in need of help, they called upon other Sikh rulers for aid; but, otherwise, they did not hesitate to support the Muslim princes".[213] This policy stood the misl in good stead and was a crucial factor in their survival to the dawn of India's independence.

Abdali's sixth invasion in 1762 left a poignant memoir of the great massacre (Vada Ghallughara). As Abdali advanced towards Lahore Jassa Singh Ahluwalia withdrew his forces and directed his soldiers and their families to seek refuge in the semi-desert sandy plain to the southwest. Abdali pursued and caught up with the fleeing families near Kup Kalan, about fifteen Km north of Maler Kotla. The Sikh soldiers formed a shield around women and children and moved towards Barnala where they expected reinforcements

---

[213] The Sikh Misls & the Panjab State by Sohan Singh Seetal p.97

from the Phulkian misl. Ala Singh, sardar of the Phulkian misl, however, was a no show. Abdali rained terror on the besieged families slaughtering them by the thousands.[214]

Latif provides an entirely different perspective. According to him, Abdali "invaded Barnala, then the chief town of Patiala, to punish the audacity of the Sikhs, who had given trouble to Zen Khan, governor of Sirhind, after his departure from India in the previous year. The Sikhs, including Phulkia chief, made common cause against the Mahomedan invader". In an intensely fought battle, Sikhs lost 20,000 men.[215]

Prompted by his drive to retain his fiefdom, Phulkian sardar courted Ahmad Shah Abdali, the Afghan scourge. Thus, during his seventh invasion in 1764, Abdali managed to tap the thick vein of Ala Singh's motivation to his own advantage by having the Phulkian sardar provide assistance to the invader; a sycophantic act that so outraged Dal Khalsa that they declared war on the Phulkian misl. Timely intervention by Jassa Singh Ahluwalia averts further tragedy (see Bhangi misl for more details).

Phulkian misl suffered from its own in-house rebellion. When Ala Singh died in 1765, his three sons

---

[214] A History of the Sikhs by Khushwant Singh – Vol. 1 p.153-154
[215] History of the Punjab by Syed Muhammad Latif published 1891 – p.327

had predeceased him and two grandsons survived him: Himmat Singh and Amar Singh. The widow of Ala Singh invested the younger brother Amar Singh as Maharaja. That so piqued Himmat Singh that he invoked the custom of primogeniture to claim the throne. However, most of the chieftains, including the Maharajas of Nabha and Jind, backed Amar Singh.

During the early years of his reign, Amar Singh was engaged in several skirmishes with his neighbours. Jodh Singh of Kot Kapura, a town some fifteen kilometers southeast of Faridkot, had crossed swords with him over some prized horses. He attacked and killed him. He captured villages owned by Baghel Singh. In 1770, he besieged Sukhchain Singh who holed up in his fort at Bhatinda. Thus, while he was fighting against Rajput Bhatti neighbours, his brother Himmat Singh seized Patiala and declared himself Maharaja. With the help of Jassa Singh Ahluwalia, Rajas of Nabha and Jind and Nawabs of Maler Kotla and Rai Kot, and several other chiefs Amar Singh prepared to dislodge his brother. Himmat Singh was awed by the overwhelming forces arrayed against him, sued for peace and was awarded a jagir (a large estate). Himmat Singh died in 1774, and thereby ended the family feud.

Two years later, in 1767, Abdali raided Punjab for the eighth time. Amar Singh, the Phulkian sardar, joined Abdali as he crossed the Sutlej into Malwa. The lackey sardar was awarded "the district of Sirhind and invested with the insignias of royalty and the title

Raja-i-Rajgan".[216] Seetal, on the other hand, sets the scene differently. According to Seetal, it was "during Abdali's ninth invasion in 1767" that Amar Singh paid a steep tribute to have Abdali "grant (him) the command of Sirhind" and bestow on him the title of Raja-i-Rajgan.[217]

Amar Singh died in 1781, at age thirty-five, of dropsy, and succeeded by his six-year-old son, Sahib Singh. De facto power now rested in the hands of a few of the royal household women, principally Rani Hukmaan, infant's grandmother; Bibi Pardhan, grand-aunt of the infant; Rajindar, a first cousin of Amar Singh and Sahib Kaur sister of the infant misldar.[218] Rani Hukmaan, infant's grandmother, appointed Manoo Mall as regent.

Manoo Mall's regency did not sit well with Bibi Pradhan but she eschewed open revolt. An opportunity to dislodge Manoo Mall came her way during the famine of 1783. The drought and starvation gave rise to riots and general unrest. Sardool Singh, infant misldar's granduncle "rose in revolt in Moolepur" and Manoo Mall set out to suppress him. During the confrontation, Manoo Mall wounded and relocated to Anandpur. At same time, Rani Hukmaan passed away. Thereupon the other woman of royal household, among them Bibi

---

[216] A History of the Sikhs by Khushwant Singh – Vol. 1 p.165
[217] The Sikh Misls & the Panjab State by Sohan Singh Seetal p.97
[218] History of the Punjab by Syed Muhammad Latif published 1891 p.328

Pradhan, seized Manoo Mall, took him captive and placed him into custody in Patiala.

This episode provoked Rani Rajindar of Phagwara, a first cousin of Amar Singh, to mobilize her forces and advance to Patiala to rescue Manoo Mall, a man she felt was the "only competent and reliable" to handle the affairs of the Phulkian misl and restored him as the regent.[219]

Manoo Mall, though an administrator extraordinaire, was also an arrogant man. He smoked in the darbar (court) and given to insolence and disrespect towards other misl sardars. He was nepotistic in the extreme by appointing his sons, nephews, and relatives to responsible posts. His behaviour led Rani Rajindar Kaur to have doubts of her own.

Matters came to a head in 1789 when the Marathas who were flexing their power in the imperial city of Delhi ventured forth into the Malwa region under the Maratha General Rani Khan to exact tribute from the Malwai misldars. Manoo Mal paid substantial portion of the tribute levied on Patiala but he wanted Rani Rajindar Kaur to cough up the balance of the tax money. This request intensified Rajinder Kaur's suspicions of Manoo Mall's motivations and she preemptively arrested his son Devi Ditta and hunkered down to face a punitive offensive by the Marathas.

---

[219] The Sikh Misls & the Panjab State by Sohan Singh Seetal p.101

An outraged Manoo Mall threw in his lot with the Marathas who advanced and encamped within sight of the city of Patiala. The shrewd Rani Rajindar Kaur reached a quid pro quo with Manoo Mall: agreeing to free Devi Ditta in return for Manoo Mall to pay the balance of the levy owed to the Marathas. To complete the transaction both Rani Rajindar Kaur and Manoo Mall proceeded to Mathra to settle the payment of tribute with General Madhaji Sindhia, a Peshwa (head of the Maratha confederacy).

While Rani Rajindar Kaur was in Mathra some of the Patiala courtiers who felt threatened by her seized the moment to poison 16 year-old Raja Sahib Singh's mind against the Rani. On her return, the Rani found herself out of the loop and subject to a cool and silent treatment from the Raja. She died in 1791 and the following year Manoo Mall, too, passed away.

Sahib Kaur, born 1771, elder sister of the infant misldar, was made "wazir and administrator". She was married to Kanhaya sardar Jaimal Singh, and imbued with a warrior like spirit that exuded a strong and forceful personality.

In 1795, Maratha General Nana Rao established his presence on the banks of Ghaggar River – a seasonal, intermittent river that originates in Shivalik hills and meanders through Ambala and Hissar before drying up in the deserts of Rajasthan. His mission was to collect the tribute due to the Marathas by the Phulkian misldar. Sahib Kaur felt it was time to curb Maratha appetite for demanding tribute and appealed to neighboring sardars to join her to repel the Marathas. Sensing defeat, following an intense daylong battle, Sikh sardars implored Sahib Kaur to retreat to Patiala. Instead, the warrior in Sahib Kaur launched out an impromptu pre-emptive night strike on the unsuspecting Marathas and routed them.[220]

Sahib Kaur did not endear herself to her sister-in-law Aas Kaur, Raja Sahib Singh's second wife. Aas Kaur probably felt that the adroit administrator and fearless warrior Sahib Kaur was usurping her husband's authority. She instigated a poisonous campaign against Sahib Kaur and succeeded in having her husband's ear. To minimize sibling fracture Sahib Kaur retired to her fiefdom in Abowal. However, this did not assuage Sahib Singh who wanted his sister Sahib Kaur to rejoin her husband Jaimal Singh, the Kanhaya sardar. Sahib Kaur simply paid no heed to her brother's dictate, which so incensed Sahib Singh that he marched with his army to attack his sister. Some sardars acted as intermediaries and Sahib Kaur agreed to accompany her brother to Patiala. Once in Patiala her brother had her taken into custody and locked up in the fort of Bhawanigarh, some 40 Km west of Patiala. She escaped disguised as a maid and returned to Abowal where she died in 1799.

The demise of Sahib Kaur, the last of the larger than life women of Patiala royal family, ended the divisiveness and infighting that had plagued the misl.

---

[220] The Sikh Misls & the Panjab State by Sohan Singh Seetal – p.103

To its credit, Phulkian misl, unlike some other misls of Dal Khalsa, had the good luck of not torn asunder by family discord.

The Phulkian misl also profited from its geographical location. Its location in the Malwa region of Cis-Sutlej placed it outside the rampaging range of the Afghan menace Ahmad Shah Abdali. Even in rare instances that Abdali loomed on the horizon, Phulkian chief avoided harm by ingratiating himself with the invader. Since Phulkian suzerainty lay outside of Punjab that was in constant state of turmoil either from without (numerous Abdali invasions) or from within (misls toppling or knocking over one another), it felt protected from harm or danger.

The Phulkian misl also benefited from the lifting of the long shadow that the Marathas had cast over their domain by exacting of heavy tributes. Although badly mauled in the final battle of Panipat in 1761 by Abdali, Marathas continued to exercise a modicum of power in the imperial city of Delhi and environs. For instance, Shah Alam ll remained "a helpless puppet in the hands of his ministers and the Marathas".[221] In 1803, the British General Lord Lake captured the imperial city of Delhi from Maratha peshwa Daulat Rao Sindhia and "Shah Alam became a pensioner of the British".[222] Phulkian chieftain paid homage to Lord Lake.

---

[221] The Mogul Empire by Ashirbadilal Srivastava – p. 438
[222] *ibid* – p.439

Shifts in power had clearly delineated the political landscape. The Phulkian misl found itself sandwiched by Maharaja Ranjit Singh in the west and the British in the east. In 1808 members of the loose knit Malwa confederacy that included sardars of Patiala, Jind, Nabha, and Kaithal approached British Resident seeking British protection.

When Maharaja Ranjit Singh got wind of what the sardars of Malwa were up to, he invited them to Amritsar for entente. He tried exchanging turbans with Raja Sahib Singh but to no avail as the Malwa confederates insisted on pledging their allegiance to the British. Consequently, the Maharaja and the British signed a treaty on April 25, 1809 establishing "Sutlej River as the boundary between the two powers" and extended British protection to Phulkian chieftain and other Rajas of Malwa".[223]

Sahib Singh died on March 26, 1813 and succeeded by his eldest son Karam Singh who remained steadfastly loyal to the British. He helped the British in the Gurkha war (1814-1816) which ended in a stalemate. He allied himself with the British during the first Sikh War of 1845. The war started a week before Christmas at Mudki – about 40 Km southeast of Ferozpur –but it was during the fiercely fought battle of Ferozshah – midway between Mudki and Ferozpur – when Karam Singh passed away on December 23.

---

[223] The Sikh Misls & the Panjab State by Sohan Singh Seetal p.105-106

Narinder, at 23, succeeded Karam Singh. He strengthened his alliance with the British even more and, in turn, amply rewarded with territorial grants of jagirs. During the mutiny of 1857, "no prince in India stood so boldly and heartily on the side of the British Government as the Maharaja of Patiala, who was the most conspicuous for his loyalty and attachment to the paramount power".[224] The British awarded several parcels of territories to him and bestowed a slew of high-sounding honorific titles e.g. awarded Star of India in 1861, nominated member of the Council of the Governor-General. He died in November 1862.

The British-Sikh treaty of 1809[225] stipulated that the Phulkian domain "shall be exempted from all pecuniary tribute to the British Government" and that the misl chieftain "shall remain in the full exercise of the same rights and authority" in his domain which he enjoyed before he was "received under the British protection".[226] That protection ensured the survival of the Phulkian misl.

---

[224] History of the Punjab by Syed Muhammad Latif published 1891 p.328
[225] The Treaty of Amritsar - a pact concluded between British East India Company and Maharaja Ranjit Singh fixing the frontier lands controlled by Ranjit Singh along the line of the Sutlej River.
[226] The Sikh Misls & the Panjab State by Sohan Singh – p. 106

Sukerchakia Misl

At the start, Sukerchakia misl was neither a large nor a powerful entity. Unlike some misls that were destroyed by in-house conspiracies or usurpers or some misls that bend knee before powerful adversaries, Sukerchakia misl survived by the courage and guile of its leaders. The misl made their home in a strategically important region - between the Ravi and Chenab, Rechna Doab – straddling Lahore (seat of Imperial power) and Amritsar (Sikhdom's holist city).

The house of Sukerchakia traces their lineal descent from one Kalu, a Hindu Jat, who lived in Pindi Bhattian, a village 110 Km North West of Lahore, 15 Km east of Chenab River. Early in life following a family quarrel he left his ancestral village around 1470 and settled down in a village Sansri, near Rajasansi, a town situated 15 Km northwest of Amritsar, a stone's throw from present day Sri Guru Ram Dass Jee International Airport.

Rajasansi and its environs that included Majitha was an area inhabited by the nomadic sansis, a tribe known for their chosen vocation of plunder and loot. Kalu's wife gave birth to a son named Jaddoman who following the death of his parents became member of the sansi tribe and actively engaged in dacoity. Jaddoman died, circa 1515, in one of the plundering expeditions and his son Galeb followed his father's example. When Galeb died in 1549, in one of his pillaging raids, his only son Kiddoh moved to Sukerchak in 1555, then a tiny hamlet near Gujranwala where he "started peaceful life of a labourer at the land".[227] Kiddoh died in 1578.

For next three generations Kiddoh's descendants extended their agricultural pursuits by going into shop keeping. Kiddoh's great grandson, Bhai Bara, greatly expanded family ownership of land. He was a pious man well versed in Granth and preached the gospel of Guru Nanak. His "dying injunction to his son (Buddha) was that he should read the holy Granth and become a Sikh, and, with this last advice to him, he died in 1679".[228]

In his adolescence, Buddha set out for Amritsar, about 1692, and received his baptism. He was the first of the family to embrace Sikhism. Unlike his father and grandfather who were farmers and shopkeepers, Buddha returned to the vocation of his forbears by collaborating with Sansi gangs and other Sikh bandits in predatory expeditions that included cattle rustling. His audacious and intrepid exploits made him the most prominently known dacoit leader.[229] He

---

[227] Punjab Through the Ages Vol ll S.R. Bakshi and Rashmi Pathak (editors) – p.12
[228] History of the Punjab by Syed Muhammad Latif published 1891 – p.336-337
[229] *Ibid* - This account by Latif at page 337 is at variance with his earlier narrative at page 282 where he writes "Desu Jat, a petty zemindar of the *Sansi* tribe, who lived in Sukerchak, a village in the Manjha country. He owned three ploughs and a well, with which he managed to eke out a living for himself and his family.

accumulated vast riches and made Sukerchak his principal abode. He died in 1716 leaving two sons: Nodh Singh and Chanda Singh, and from the latter the "Sindhianwala branch of the family, related to the Maharaja on the mother's side, sprang".[230]

Nodh Singh discovered that rustling cattle was less rewarding than brigandry. It was a time when banditry had no stigma attached to it and was a way of life that appealed to Nodh Singh who henceforward set his sights on brigandry. He led his gang on raids countrywide, often to the edges of the Sutlej River. His fame spread, his expeditions made him a hero, and he amassed a lot of treasure.

Nodh Singh gained stature as a feared leader. In 1730, he married the daughter of Gulab Singh, a Sansi Jat, who was one of the important chiefs of Majithia. He joined the Fyzulpuria misl also known as Singhpuria misl, founded by Kapur Singh.[231] This association began during Ahmad Shah Abdali's first invasion of India in 1747 when the Sikh misls pounced on the booty-laden Abdali caravan that was homeward bound to Afghanistan. Nodh Singh enriched himself with the spoils and honoured as the chief of Sukerchak. Nodh Singh enriched himself with the

---

He had a son Nodh Singh". From this contradiction, one can only deduce that Desu and Buddha is the same person.
[230] *ibid.* – p.337
[231] Kapur Singh had captured the village of Fyzullapur from its Muslim founder Fyzullah and although he renamed the village Singhpur, some people still referred to it by its former name of Fyzulpur

spoils and honoured as the chief of Sukerchak. The same year, an Afghan shot him and incapacitated him. Nodh Singh died in 1752 and survived by four sons: Charat, Dal, Chet, and Mangi. Mangi Singh, the youngest son, chose to live a very ascetic life and died childless. Charat Singh, born in 1721, figured out that he could do much better on his own and decided to break away from the Fyzulpuria misl. He persuaded his two remaining brothers to do likewise.

The brothers formed their own independent band and moved their headquarters from Sukerchak to Rajasansi, returning to the home of their forebears. They were able to tap into the Sansi tribe and other kindred spirits to organize into a formidable force of 150-armed horsemen. They roamed across the "adjoining tracts of country on plundering excursions (and) took forcible possession of all the villages in the neighborhood of Gujranwala".[232]

In 1756, Charat Singh married the daughter of Amir Singh of Gujranwala. Amir Singh belonged to the Sansi tribe and his family was devoted to the Sikh faith. He was once a member of the Fyzulpuria misl and like Charat Singh, he, too, diverged from that misl to strike out on his own. He gained notoriety for his plundering raids and he acquired large tracts of estate in Gujranwala and environs. The marriage cemented the family bonds and together the two sardars formed their own misl, known as Sukerchakia

---

[232] History of the Punjab by Syed Muhammad Latif published 1891 – p.338

misl, a name derived from Sukerchak, once the stronghold of Charat's grandfather Buddha Singh. Although the two sardars were co-leaders, the aging Amir Singh let Charat Singh be the de facto leader.

Charat Singh sacked Eminabad, located 15 Km south of Gujranwala, killed city's Mogul faujdar, and carried away a good deal of spoils and arsenal. The Muslim chiefs of Lahore, who had been watching the Sikh activities became apprehensive of the rising sphere of control of the Sikhs, allied together (circa 1777) and "moved with a strong force to destroy their strongholds and disperse their bands (but) the invading army was completely routed".[233]

Following Ahmad Shah Abdali's sixth invasion in 1762, Charat Singh conquered one Mogul city after another. His serial sacking of Wazirabad, Ahmadabad, Rohtas, Dhanni, Chakwal, Jalalpur, Kot Sahib Khan and Raja-ka-kot made him the envy of rival misldars who in the words of Antisthenes were "as iron is eaten by rust, so are the envious consumed by envy". These other misldars felt insecure and threatened, none more so than the Bhangi misl chieftain Jhanda Singh.

---

[233] History of the Punjab by Syed Muhammad Latif published 1891 - p.339 .....from this time the audacity of the Sikhs increased, and they began to organize themselves into a still more compact and formidable body under Charat Singh, who, as his fame increased, established his power as the head of the Sukerchakia misl.

Matters came to a head in the conflict over the right of succession to the state of Jammu (1774), which saw Sukerchakia misl forces arrayed against the Bhangi misl (details of the encounter are narrated under Bhangi misl section). During the hostilities one of his own soldiers accidentally killed Charat Singh. He shepherded emergence of Sikh dominance.[234].

Maha Singh, the ten-year-old son of Charat Singh succeeded him. Being a minor and not old enough to manage the vast holdings that he inherited and, too young to command the misl, his mother, Desan, assumed the regency, with Jai Singh of Kanhaya misl as advisor. In 1774, Maha Singh married his betrothed fiancé, Raj Kaur, the daughter of Gajpat Singh, Raja of Jind.

Maha Singh was to prove his mettle as a worthy commander when he embarked on his endeavour to recover the famous zamzama gun. Jai Singh sardar of Kanhaya misl had captured the gun from Ahmad Shah abdali and given its custody to Pir Mahomed, a member of the powerful Jat tribe of Chatthas, and chief of Rassulnagar, a town located on the east bank of Chenab River (see Kanhaya misl section for details).

Aware that the city of Rassulnagar was heavily fortified, Maha Singh, sardar of Sukerchakia misl,

---

[234] ibid – p.340 – he appeared early in the field as an enterprising leader and soon rose from a common Dharwi, or highway robber, to the sardari of a confederacy, and contributed materially to the strength of the Sikhs as a nation.

assisted by Jai Singh, the Kanhaya chief, at the head of 6,000 troops set up a blockade of the city intent upon conquering it by attrition or assault. Also aware that Chatthas occupied several towns and villages in area surrounding the city of Rassulnagar, from Marh Chattha 25 Km in the south-east to Jamke Chattha about 10 Km linearly east, Maha Singh systematically ravaged them with their farmed fields laid waste. The Chatthas had friendly ties with the Bhangi chiefs but were unable to secure their aid, as the Bhangis were busy in their conquest of Multan, a city only second to Lahore as seat of Mogul power. The siege lasting four months forced the Chatthas to surrender. The sons of Pir Mahomed put to death and the city saw wide spread looting. The conquest of Rassulnagar made Maha Singh a household name impelling other sardars, who had hitherto been Bhangi sycophants, to swear allegiance to him.[235]

Maha Singh made it his mission to subdue all other misls still extant at the time. Fortuitous events helped him set his sights on Bhangi power. Taimur Shah had mortally wounded Bhangi misl, the largest, and the most dominant of the misls, when he dislodged them from their bastion of Multan and Bahawalpur. The leading Bhangi chief Desa Singh spent his life in debauch. Smelling out weakening of Bhangi power,

---

[235] History of the Punjab by Syed Muhammad Latif published 1891 – p.340-341 – sardars transferred their allegiance to him, and deemed it an honour to fight under his banner......relics of the prophet Mahomed, which fell into the hands of the victors in their sack of Rassulnagar, were removed by Maha Singh to Gujranwala and deposited there in proper custody.

Maha Singh attacked and seized possessions of Bhangi sardars such as Pindi Bhattian, Jhang, Musa Khel, and other places.

Maha Singh then advanced eastwards and captured Kotli Loharan, a town 10 Km northeast of Sailkot, well known for its arms manufacture (matchlocks). While there he invited leading sardars on the pretext of convening a general counsel and at their gathering, he placed most of them in custody and only released them on payment of a tribute.

His modus operandi was to gobble up town after town and to chasten and humiliate their sardars. Misldars were in such awe of him that rather than put up resistance they simply capitulated. As his commonwealth grew and other sardars cowered, he set his sights on Jammu, a prosperous city of note.

Jammu had a particular troubling memory for Maha Singh. In 1774 rebellion by heir-apparent Brij Raj Dev to topple his father that pitted Sukerchakai misl (on behalf of the son) against Bhangi misl (supporting the father), not only Charat Singh, Maha Singh's father, die during the hostilities but the Bhangi misl had seized some of the territory, an image deeply imprinted on Maha Singh's mind.

On his ascension, Brij Raj Dev sought to recover his lost possessions in the hands of the Bhangi misl and appealed to Haqiqat Singh, a Kanhaya sardar, for assistance. Following the recovery of Karianwala, a town 25 Km northeast of Sailkot, Kanhaya sardar switched sides and joined the Bhangis and together they plotted to invade Jammu. Brij Raj Dev now appealed to Maha Singh for help. In the ensuing battle, Bhangi-Kanhaya forces routed the Sukerchakia chief and the forlorn raja submitted to paying a tribute to Haqiqat Singh.

When the Jammu raja dawdled over the payment, Haqiqat Singh invited Maha Singh for a joint invasion of Jammu. The city was looted and torched and the countryside desolated. In a Machiavellian way Maha Singh took over supreme command to the chagrin of Haqiqat Singh and before the latter could square up to Maha Singh he died.

In 1783, Maha Singh visited Amritsar, a Kanhaya misl stronghold, to perform ablution. This was soon after his sacking of Jammu that had enriched him immensely and made him the envy of the Bhangi sardars; who, in turn, succeeded in "excit(ing) a strong jealousy in the mind of Jai Singh" - the Kanhaya misl chief once the "guardian and ally" of Maha Singh. That prompted Jai Singh to insult the youthful Maha Singh while he was paying homage to him. Incensed by his humiliation, Maha Singh vowed to avenge the insult and called upon Jassa Singh Ramgarhia to mount a joint attack on the Kanhaya chieftain. Jassa Singh readily obliged as he bore a grudge against the Kanhaya misl for expelling him from the doabs and now hoped to recover his lost possessions.

Following year, in 1784, forces led by Maha Singh and Jassa Singh Ramgarhia met the Kanhaya misl forces led by Gurbaksh Singh, son of Jai Singh, at a battlefield near Batala. Gurbaksh Singh died in fierce fighting and seeing their leader dead the Kanhayias made a speedy retreat.[236]

This was the beginning of the end of Kanhaya misl: Jai Singh went into seclusion and passed the baton to Sada Kaur, his daughter–in-law, who was to cement the relationships between the two misls by the betrothal of her daughter to Maha Singh's heir Ranjit Singh (for more detail, refer to the sketch on Kanhaya misl).

Maha Singh died in 1792 and succeeded by Ranjit Singh. By that time the bloom of Bhangi misl had begun to fade; more so, after the death of its illustrious chief Gujjar Singh.[237] The Bhangi leadership passed to sons who were pygmies compared to their forebears, a succession of weakened men who indulged in carpe diem debauch. Ranjit Singh took advantage of the situation and one by one he subdued them (for more detail, refer to the Bhangi misl section).

While Charat Singh laid the cornerstone of the house of Sukerchakia by capturing more territory in less time than any other misldar and amassing much more

---

[236] History of the Punjab by Syed Muhammad Latif published 1891 – p. 343-344

[237] The year Gujjar Singh died is in dispute. According to Latif (p.304) following his bequeathal to his youngest son Fateh Singh, Gujjar Singh retired to Lahore where he died in 1788 while Seetal at page 27 states that he died in 1791.

treasure that made him the envy of leading misl chieftains of his time, it rested on his son, Maha Singh, to assert his supremacy over much of Punjab and to subdue rival misldars. He engaged in several encounters with the other misl sardars and eventually subdued them.

In his quest for domination, Maha Singh faced extreme dangers and difficulties without fear. Known for military stratagem, he proved his mettle in combat. He was a strict disciplinarian and a critical thinker and admired for political shrewdness. On some moral issues, he was uncompromising as is evident in his killing his mother whom he suspected of adulterous affair with Haqiqat Singh, a Kanhaya sardar. Word had it that he suspected his own wife, mother of Ranjit Singh, of illicit liaison The matricide, however, weighed so heavily on his conscience that he took to hard drinking.

As he accumulated power and authority over fellow misldars, he realized that the zeitgeist, which promoted banditry, was passé and that exercise of effective power rested on political power. This sea change in thinking urged him to adopt tactics geared to seize and occupy territory over which he can exercise rule and control. His skills as an astute leader with farsighted goals endeared him to all people.

Maha Singh died in 1792 and chieftainship of Sukerchakia misl passed on to his 12-year old son, Ranjit Singh, who inherited "a large district in the heart of Punjab", headquartered in Gujranwala, about

70 Km north of Lahore.[238] As Ranjit Singh was a minor, his mother held the regency. However, his mother-in-law Sada Kaur was not without influence.

Sada Kaur was an exceptionally artful and adroit woman who is credited with all of Ranjit Singh's early exploits and "was the ladder by which Ranjit Singh reached the summit if his power".[239] In return, on the passing of Kanhaya sardar Jai Singh in 1793, Ranjit Singh helped Sada Kaur take control of Kanhaya misl.

Ranjit Singh had little or no schooling. He spent his early years hunting and youthful indiscretions. Maha Singh thought highly of his son who "had accompanied him on several expeditions" and seeing his son's "courage and aptitude", once remarked, "the state of Gujranwala will not be a sufficient kingdom for my son. He will one day carve out a great empire for himself".[240]

An attack of smallpox had left Ranjit Singh scarred and sightless in one eye. In his book Bakshi quotes Griffin on Ranjit Singh, writing "although short of stature and disfigured by that cruel disease was the beau ideal of soldier, strong, spare, active, courageous and enduring. An excellent horseman, he would

---

[238] A History of the Sikhs by Khushwant Singh – p. 188
[239] History of the Punjab by Syed Muhammad Latif published 1891 – p.346
[240] Punjab Through the Ages Vol ll S.R. Bakshi and Rashmi Pathak (editors) – p.23-24

remain the whole day in saddle without showing any sign of fatigue".[241]

At the behest of his guardians, he married Raj Kaur, daughter of Ram Singh, chief of Nakkai misl. She gave birth to Kharak Singh.

In 1799, at age 17, Ranjit Singh took over the reins of the misl and appointed Dal Singh, his great-uncle, as his wazir (political advisor). He suspected his mother of love affairs. One day when informed by a servant that she was entertaining her paramour he hurried to her boudoir to find his mother half-naked. Although the lover made his escape, he had left behind articles of his clothing. In a blinding rage, he unsheathed his sword and killed his mother on the spot.[242]

---

[241] Punjab Through the Ages Vol ll S.R. Bakshi and Rashmi Pathak (editors) – p.24

[242] Dr. Gopal Singh strongly discounts this account of matricide by Syed Muhammad Latif (page 347). Dr. Gopal Singh believes that "these scandals and canards are generally spread by the losers against a successful rival, in order to sow the seeds of disaffection against him and to bring him down in public estimation". Dr. Gopal Singh then added, "That Carmichael Smyth in his 'History of the Reigning Family of Lahore' accuses Ranjit's father also with matricide for her (sic) mother's intimacy with Hakikat Singh". In addition, Dr. Gopal Singh feels some of the British historians of the period were determined on character assassination of the entire family of Ranjit Singh; their principal rival in India in the first half of the nineteenth century" at page 441 of his book "A History of the Sikh People".

From early on, Ranjit Singh realized that he who controlled Lahore held imperia over Punjab. Throughout the ages, Lahore was a city of record. A tenth century Persian writer referred to it as a shahr (city) with "temples, large markets, and huge orchards". It was a prized gem in the Mogul crown, whose governorship coveted by top members of the inner circle of Mogul emperor.

Its strategic location placed Lahore directly in the path of the invaders; the city won and lost repeatedly. The Mogul hold on the city lasted longest but as the Afghan sensed the Mogul empire was beginning to wane the Afghan ruler Ahmad Shah Abdali descended upon northern India regularly, as did his descendents Timur Shah and Shah Zaman. However, as soon as the Afghan turned homeward bound or driven out, the Sikh misls would fill in the void and occupy Lahore until forced to vacate by the next wave of Afghan invasion.

In 1796, Zaman Shah Durrani, son of Timur Shah, invaded India for the fourth time. The Bhangi sardars who held Lahore vacated the city, as was their habit. This time around, the misldars adopted guerilla warfare against the Afghans that so tired Shah Zaman that, in January 1799, he abandoned Lahore and returned to Kabul. As word reached that he had forded Ravi River the Bhangi sardars re-occupied Lahore.

In 1799, Ranjit Singh severed Bhangi hold over Lahore and took possession of the city (see Bhangi misl for details). Prior to the assault on Lahore, Ranjit Singh had issued a firman (decree) to his troops that forbade looting and ill-treatment of the citizenry of Lahore. Nevertheless, anticipating widespread looting businesses had shuttered their stores. After his triumphant capture of the city, Ranjit Singh assured the inhabitants of Lahore of fair and just treatment and protection of life and liberty from outside aggressors. City life returned to normal and acknowledged his overlordship.

However, rival sardars in neighboring territories seethed with resentment and anger. They formed an alliance – consisting of Gulab Singh, Bhangi sardar of Amritsar; Sahib Singh, Bhangi sardar of Gujrat, Jodh Singh representing his aging father Jassa Singh Ramgarhia - to oust Ranjit Singh. In early 1800 the allied forces "marched from Amritsar under the command of their respective chiefs" to face the armies of Ranjit Singh that was reinforced by a contingent supplied by Sada Kaur at Mouza Bhasin some 16 Km east of Lahore. "A few skirmishes during the period of two months did not decide the issue. The sudden death of a powerful confederate Gulab Singh of Bhangi misl on account of hard drinking was the cause of the breakup of the confederacy (and) led to the final retreat of the combined forces".[243]

---

[243] Punjab Through the Ages Vol ll S.R. Bakshi and Rashmi Pathak (editors)– – p. 37

Thereafter, Ranjit Singh held undisputed suzerainty over Lahore; a city that was a hub of imperial power in the Punjab for both the Moguls and the Afghans. His occupation of Lahore catapulted him into the limelight and "created awe and fear in the minds of the other chiefs of the misls". However, chiefs of other misls were wedded to the 'I'm-all-right, Jack' syndrome. Their self-interest engendered by deep suspicion of one another impeded unity. Ranjit Singh exploited the schism by playing one against the other, forcing some to paying tribute and overthrowing the recalcitrant.[244]

In 1801, Ranjit Singh held a darbar, attended by all chiefs, sardars, tributaries, and prominent citizens who had pledged allegiance to him, at which he proclaimed himself Maharaja, and a coin struck in commemoration.

The city of Amritsar was one prize that eluded Ranjit Singh. Amritsar embodied the soul of the Sikh people and held in no less reverence by the Sikh collectivity than the Vatican is by the Christians. It was also a thriving commercial centre and at the time was a fiefdom of Bhangi misl. A minor, Gurdit Singh, son of Gulab Singh, under the regency of his mother Mai Sukhan, ruled it.

---

[244] The Sikhs by Patwant Singh – p.107: Ranjit Singh's consolidation of his control over Punjab continued with the annexation of the Karorsinghia, Singhpuria and Dallewalia *misls*. The circumstances of each of these differed; one was absorbed on the death of a chief, another through conquest, yet another through negotiation.

Ranjit Singh set his heart to dislodge the Bhangis. With the help of Fateh Singh, sardar of Ahluwalia misl in particular and misldars of Kanahya and Nakkai misls he besieged the city and forced the capitulation of the Bhangi (circa 1802).

The acquisition of Amritsar made Ranjit Singh the sole power in Chaj, Rechna, and Bari Doabs. In other words, he was the undisputed overlord of the territory encased within Rivers Jhelum and Sutlej. He feared no enemy from within or faced threat from without, as the Afghan kings had given up any hope of hegemony over Punjab. He now looked eastwards at Bist Doab to expand his domain.

The four misls: Ahluwalia, Ramgarhia, Singhpuria, and Dallewalia divided the territory between Rivers Beas and Sutlej (i.e. Bist Doab) among them. The estates owned by these sardars were not contiguous; the villages and towns intermingled because of haphazard acquisition.

For example, in 1769, the Ahluwalia territory straddled the River Beas but most of it was located east of Beas hugging the northwestern part of Doaba-Jullundur. Ramgarhia, too, straddled River Beas owning a good chunk of northern parts of Bist Doab and possessed Batala, Dina Nagar in Bari Doab. Singhpuria misl held territory around both Ludhiana and Abohar. Dallewalia misl occupied Ropar and areas southeast of Ambala.

Ranjit Singh had no designs on conquering territories occupied by the Ahluwalia misl, as he had exchanged turbans with the Ahluwalia sardar, Fateh Singh, signifying perpetual brotherly bonds, and, therefore, left them untouched. As far as Ramgarhia misl was concerned Ranjit Singh ended their imperium over the Doabs at the battle of Batala in 1796 (the event is detailed in the sketch on Ramgarhia misl).

Budh Singh, chief of Singhpuria misl, did not consider himself beholden to Ranjit Singh and, therefore, when summoned to Lahore in 1811, he balked at the very idea of beckoning. Ranjit Singh was irritated. To punish the recalcitrant sardar, he mobilized and dispatched an army comprising Ahluwalia and Ramgarhia misls to attack Budh Singh. After some days of fighting, Budh Singh fled to Ludhiana to seek British protection and Ranjit Singh confiscated his territories.

Gulab Singh founded the Dallewalia misl in 1748. He pillaged and accumulated vast riches that helped him maintain a large army of nearly 10,000 horsemen. He died without a son and succeeded by a relative, Gurdial Singh, who died on battlefield the following year. Tara Singh of village Torawali succeeded Gurdial Singh. Ranjit Singh charged Fateh Singh, chief of Ahluwalia misl, to attack the Dallewalias who suffered a devastating defeat resulting in confiscation of their possessions. Tara Singh died in 1807 whereupon Ranjit Singh pensioned off his descendants.

Ranjit Singh now held absolute power over Punjab. His ambitions to conquer Malwa region in southern Punjab lying in the east of River Beas, that included cities like Ludhiana, Patiala, Ambala, Karnal, Sangrur, Malerkotla, Shahabad, and Abohar, wa thwarted.

7. SUKERCHAKIA juggernaut crushes all adversaries

The misls were motley of competing interest groups in their infancy. The raison d'être of each group or band (Jatha) was identical, which was for a career as marauders and highwaymen. Individual Jathas would stake out their territories for prowling around in search of loot and plunder.

The drive to extend their sphere of control as far wide as possible prompted individual Jatha to radiate from its native habitat to lay claims on villages and towns willy-nilly. Possessions, therefore, were haphazardly acquired and not always contiguous.

In time, they changed their tactics. Instead of terrorizing the villages and towns, they offered them protection (rakhi) against interlopers and in return exact some form of tithe. As a misl amassed large treasure, it also attracted greater following. The stronger misls would flex their muscles and intimidate the weaker ones.

Factional fighting and splits over personality thus caused rifts between misls. The rise of one misl immediately countered by a coalition of its rivals, as was a boundary dispute or unwillingness to share spoils or avenging of a perceived insult. An illustration of this is the dispute between Kanhaya and

Ramgrahia misldars over territories straddling River Beas that induced Ahluwalia sardar to join forces with the Kanhaya misldar Jai Singh. Badly beaten no vestige of Ramgrahia misl presence remained in the Doab - driven out, and forced to relocate to Hissar (see Kanhaya misl for details).

Additionally, in-house conspiracies plagued some misl. The Bhangi misl provides a typical example. The quarrels among three Bhangi siblings – sons of Bhangi misldar Gujjar Singh - over family estate became so fierce that it resulted in the fratricide of one brother and stripping of another of his property (see Bhangi misl for more details).

Like the Roman gladiators who faced violent confrontations with other gladiators, the misldars engaged in their own warfare with rival misldars that sometimes ended in the slaying of the adversary. For instance, in 1784, Kanhaya misl faced the combined forces of Sukerchakia and Ramgarhia misls in a battle fought near Batala, during which Gurbaksh Singh, son of Kanhaya misl chieftain Jai Singh, killed in action.

In the ultimate analysis fortunes of a misl rested on the derring-do of its warlord. Often successive leaders descended to dissipated living or so feeble and unstable that they failed to inspire great enthusiasm and devotion among the followers. That was a favourable omen to the opportunist misldar to seize the moment to overthrow a rival.

Ranjit Singh was to capitalize on the misls that were on the wane. A long-standing blood feud between Jassa Singh sardar of Ramgarhia misl and Sada Kaur, chief of Kanhaya misl reached its climax when a frustrated Sada Kaur beseeched Ranjit Singh to come to her aid. Consequently, in 1796, the combined forces of Kanhaya-Sukerchakia misls attacked Batala forcing Jassa Singh Ramgarhia to vacate Punjab for the last time and flee to Hissar.

Three years later, in 1799, Ranjit Singh with the help of Sada Kaur, leader of Kanhaya misl, captured Lahore from Bhangi misldar Chet Singh. Promptly he came under attack from the confederate forces of Bhangi, Ramgarhia and Nawab of Kasur intent upon dislodging him. He prevailed over them at the battle of Bhasin.

Ranjit Singh's victory at Bhasin enhanced his image, elevating his stature as the supreme misldar of Punjab. He adopted the distinctive Mogul behaviour of holding durbar (court) which led people to pay obeisance to him as a de facto ruler. He hesitated to adopt the title Maharaja fearful that it may so outrage other misldars as to prompt them to engineer a coup. However, for the same reason he wanted to project an image of a people who had thrown off the shackles of Muslim tyranny. He wanted to breathe pride into his diverse population of Punjabiness.

Finally, Ranjit Singh ended his vacillation and anointed Maharaja on propitious Baisakhi day 1801.

Sahib Singh Bedi "daubed Ranjit Singh's forehead with saffron paste and proclaimed him Maharaja of the Punjab".[245] However, he disdained wearing of royal regalia or sit on a throne. Instead, he stuck to his peasant heritage to help him cultivate the citizenry.

The assumption of the role of Maharaja of Punjab was presumptuous given that Amritsar, the holy city of the Sikhs and a key commercial center, did not fall under his suzerainty. Bhangi sardar was ensconced in Amritsar. Also, there were pockets of territories under the control of other misldars (e.g. Dallewalian misl occupied Jullundur Doab; Singhpuria misl controlled Attal Garh, Adampur, Banga in Bist Doab; Nakkai misl held Faridbad, Gugera, Sher Garh in Bari Doab).

It was not until three years later, in 1804, that Ranjit Singh with the support of Fateh Singh, sardar of Ahluwalia misl, captured Amritsar from Bhangi misldar Gurdit Singh, thereby decimating the Bhangi misl.[246]

Ranjit Singh's bonds with two misls, namely Ahluwalia misl and Kanhaya misl, were special. He was aware of the uniqueness of Ahluwalia misl. Its illustrious leader Jassa Singh was not just the chieftain

---

[245] A History of the Sikhs by Khushwant Singh – Vol. 1 p.200; It is incomprehensive how Ranjit Singh, a baptized Sikh, submitted to a Brahminical ritual in total disregard of his vows of Khalsa. For those who credit Ranjit Singh for his secularism, the ceremonial rite is an antithesis of temporal governance.
[246] for more detail refer to the sketch on Bhangi misl

of the misl; he was also the supreme commander of the Dal Khalsa army who had notched scores of victories against the Mogul and Afghan. At critical junctures, Jassa Singh was a much sought after arbiter of factional disputes. Moreover, there was also a vow of mutual fidelity and trust by a ceremony involving exchange of turbans between Ranjit Singh and Fateh Singh Ahluwalia.[247]

Ranjit Singh's relationship with Kanhaya misl was also one-of-a-kind. On the passing of the great Kanhaya misldar Jai Singh in 1798, his daughter-in-law, Sada Kaur, took over the reins of the misl. Her daughter Mehatb Kaur was married to Ranjit Singh. Ranjit Singh owed a debt of gratitude to Sada Kaur for her help in the capture Lahore. She was a politically perceptive person and one who had earned the respect of Ranjit Singh.[248]

For reasons stated, Ranjit Singh gave those two misls considerable latitude; and, largely left them alone.

---

[247] Bhag Singh, the great-grandson of Jassa Singh's uncle Gurbaksh Singh succeeded Jassa Singh who did not have a son. Fateh Singh was Bhag Singh's son (Seetal at page 82). According to Latif: the two young chieftains of Sukerchakia misl (Ranjit Singh) and Ahluwalia misl (Fateh Singh) "swore perpetual friendship on the sacred Granth and exchanged turbans in token of brotherhood" - History of the Punjab by Syed Muhammad Latif published 1891 p.317

[248] History of the Sikhs by J.D. Cunningham – p.158: "The support of Sada Kaur was of great use to Ranjit Singh in the beginning of his career, and the cooperation of Kanhaya misl mainly enabled him to master Lahore and Amritsar".

However, he saw other misls through a different prism.

The capture of Lahore, once the imperial capital of Punjab, and Amritsar, the holy city of the Sikhs, energized Ranjit Singh, chief of Sukerchakia misl, and he was hell-bent on overthrowing weakling misldars and annexing their territories.

By 1811, he had subdued remnants of misls still in possession of enclaves within Punjab, namely Dallewallian, Singhpuria, and Nakkai misls. He had secured land between Jhelum and Sutlej Rivers and was now the undisputed raja of Punjab.[249] He was an insatiate leader whose eyes now looked eastwards of Sutlej River. He coveted Malwa, a region that had a strong presence of Sikh misls, which until now remained shielded by their geographical location.

In the opening decade of nineteenth century, sardars of Malwa were in a state of extreme anxiety. On the one hand, they felt menaced from the west by Ranjit Singh who was on their doorstep. On the other hand, they were made uncomfortable by the British (East India Company) breathing down their neck from the east.[250]

---

[249] However Singhpuria misl continued to hold onto their territories in Malwa (e.g. Abohar and Bharat Garh) and likewise Dhallewallian misls (e.g. Mustafabad, Garhi, Haibatpur, Khera)

[250] The Marathas at one time exercised a powerful presence in Punjab (e.g., in 1759 they had established direct rule over Lahore). But, they were crushed at the final battle of Panipat in

Ranjit Singh had twice before crossed Sutlej River into Malwa at the head of a large army not with intent to subdue anyone but on an invitation to adjudicate inter-misl disputes.[251] Although the Malwa misldars had pledged their loyalty to Ranjit Singh they still harboured ambivalent feelings about him. Ranjit Singh used their allegiance to promote his political advantage in the Malwa to stave off British influence in the region.

He proclaimed himself the monarch of all Sikhs. However, that was an empty claim because, in 1805, after the British had chased off Marathas, Ranjit Singh was so fearful of British annexing Punjab that he conceded his suzerainty did not extend beyond the Sutlej River.

1761 and driven out of Punjab. They continued to hold sway over the Mogul Emperor Shah Alam. In 1803, Lord Lake captured the imperial city of Delhi and Shah Alam became a pensioner of the British.

[251] Not everything was hunky-dory between the Malwa misldars and often one misldar or another became a storm petrel, as happened betwixt Patiala and Nabha sardars over the ownership of village Daladi. Even though the Phulkian misl chief overpowered Nabha, the dispute was not resolved and the two parties appealed to Ranjit singh to adjudicate the matter. Ranjit Singh crossed Sutlej River with an army of twenty-thousand and the sardars all along his route welcomed him warmly. He arrived in Patialaa and adjudicated the dispute, following which all the gathered Malwa sardars swore allegiance to him. Ranjit Singh was once again invited (circa 1807) to Patiala; this rime by As Kaur, wife of Phulkian misldar Sahib Singh, to intercede in a family quarrel involving succession.

In 1807, Ranjit Singh felt that following their expedition against the Marathas the British had become a spent force and no longer the threat that he had perceived. He tasked his general Mokham Chand to wade into Malwa. Mokham Chand crossed Sutlej River and dispossessed Tara Singh Gheba, Dhallewalian sardar, of his territories. That was a pivotal moment putting fear in the hearts of other Cis-Sutlej misldars that they would be the next target.

The chasm between Ranjit Singh and the Malwa sardars was profound. Ranjit Singh was wedded to the notion of nationalism. He wanted to establish and protect a homeland for the Sikhs. Equally, he wanted other ethnic groups to lead normal lives and maintain their culture and individual identity. He was shrewd enough to locate and determine the prevailing currents of the feelings of his subjects, which guided him to strike a balance between giving Khalsa prominence (army) and cultivating a spirit of multiculturalism (governance). On their part, the Malwa chiefs accustomed to absolute monarchical rule did not want to kowtow to Ranjit Singh.[252]

---

[252] According to Khushwant Singh (A History of the Sikhs by Khushwant Singh – Vol. 1 p.221-222): A venerable patriarch summed up their view in the following words: "We do not have a very long life, as both the British and Ranjit Singh mean to swallow us up. But whereas British protection will be like consumption, which takes a long time to kill, Ranjit Singh's advent will be like a stroke of paralysis which will destroy us within a few hours".

A delegation of Malwa chiefs assured the British Resident at Delhi of their pledge of loyalty to the British. The British listened but did not pursue the matter. Ranjit Singh took Malwa chief's betrayal as a personal affront and summoned them to Amritsar. He coaxed them into believing that he had no plans to appropriate their territories.

The British wary of French plans to invade India were too preoccupied to spare any thoughts on acceding to pleas of the Malwa chiefs. They chose to prevaricate. Ranjit Singh continued to convince the British of his legitimacy over Malwa chiefs. He even exchanged turbans with Sahib Singh, Phulkian misldar, to convince the British that he was the undisputed overlord of the entire region between the Sutlej and Jamna Rivers.

Talks between the British and Ranjit Singh went on endlessly with proposals going back and forth. The British took measure of the man convinced that Ranjit Singh talks the talk but does not walk the walk. On February 9, 1809, the British made no bones about establishing Sutlej River as demarcation of the border.[253] Ranjit Singh succumbed and signed the Anglo-Sikh Treaty of Amritsar (1809).[254]

---

[253] According to Khushwant Singh (A History of the Sikhs – Vol. 1 p.228-229): the British issued a formal proclamation "to signify the pleasure of the British government" motivated solely by the desire "to confirm the friendship with the Maharaja and to prevent any injury to his country". However, "the troops of

8– HEGEMONY OVER PUNJAB -
Afghans, Marathas & Sikhs battle it out

Sixteenth century southern India was a battlefield that pitted the Moguls against the Afghan sultanate in a jockeying for hegemony over the Deccan region.[255] Competing powers, principally Bijapur sultans and the Moguls carved up the Deccan territory, and the ownership of the respective territories was in constant flux as they fought each other for absolute dominion over the region. Into this crucible of war, the Marathas interjected themselves and as they owed

---

the Maharaja shall never advance into the country of the chiefs situated on this side of the river".

[254] Mr. Charles Theophilus Metcalfe signed this treaty, on behalf of British Government and Maharaja Ranjit Singh at Amritsar on April 25, 1809. According to this Treaty, Ranjit Singh was to recognize the river Satluj as the boundary and to accept the British suzerainty over his vassals across the river, and the English were to recognize the Maharaja as the sole sovereign on his side of River Satluj.

[255] The Deccan plateau is a vast expanse of flat terrain. It is sandwiched between the Western Ghats - a 1600 Km range that begins south of Tapi River (Gujarat-Maharsahtra border) and runs along the western seaboard merging into the Nilgri Mountains in Tamil Naidu - and the Eastern Ghats – a range that begins near Jamshedpur (West Bengal), and runs disjointedly along the eastern seaboard and, it too, merges into the Nilgri Mountains. Imagine an irregular triangle with its apex in Nilgri and the base from the Gulf of Khambhat to Jamshedpur.

loyalty to none they joined forces with whichever power would help advance their cause of Maratha homeland.

Akbar was at Kalanaur, about 25 Km west of Gurdaspur, in Punjab when he got the news of the death of his father Humayun. This prompted Adil Shah based at Chunar, a town about 30 Km south west of Varanasi, to task Hemu, his Hindu Prime Minister and chief of army, to seize the Mogul power centers of Agra and Delhi.[256] In a whirlwind of pre-emptive strikes, Hemu captured all the territory from Agra to the Sutlej River and in October 1556 enthroned himself as emperor in the fort of Delhi. The news of the fall of the epicenter of their power caused the Moguls to mobilize their forces and engage Hemu in a battle on the field of Panipat in November of 1556. During fierce fighting an arrow pierced Hemu's eye and as he fell unconscious his men believing their leader had died lost their nerve and fled in disarray.

When Akbar ascended the Mogul throne, his domain was limited to the north of India, principally Punjab. His ambition was to establish dominion over the length and breadth of the land and become a de facto ruler of Hindustan. To achieve his goal he embarked on imperial conquests, starting with his 1561

---

[256] Adil Shah was an Afghan soldier of fortune. For over three hundred years, from 1490, Yusuf Adil Shahi dynasty ruled the Sultanate of Bijapur, occupying south-east of the Deccan plateau (now part of Karnataka).

conquering of Malwa, a region east of Gujarat and south of Rajasthan. In the next thirty-four years he conquered territory after territory and after his 1595 acquisition of Kandhar, Akbar was the undisputed overlord of northern half of Hindustan. However, that was not enough as he coveted the south central regions comprising Khandesh, parts of Ahmadnagar and the Muslim ruled states of Bijapur, Bidar, Berar and Golkunda in the Deccan plateau. He made it an imperial imperative to conquer these states if he was to be the ruler of the whole of Hindustan. At the time of his death, in 1605, Akbar had captured Khandesh and part of Ahmadnagar.[257]

The control of the Deccan states remained an entrenched Mogul policy of all successive Mogul rulers. The favoured prince or heir-apparent cut their military teeth at the Deccan plateau as part of grooming for succession. It was also customary to appoint a pretender to the throne to governorship of the Deccan, dispatching him farthermost from Delhi in order to neutralize his capability to stir up rebellion.

Wielding of military imperium on the sultanates was the paramount responsibility of the Mogul governor.
While the weaker sultanates succumbed to the superior Mogul forces, some put up resistance, albeit half-heartedly, before signing a treaty exacting heavy tribute from them. However, the treaty obligations

---

[257] The Mogul Empire by Ashirbadilal Srivastava – p. 271

were seldom observed by the stronger sultanates (e.g. Bijapur), which would impel Moguls to dispatch a force to maraud the sultanate.

The Marathas populated the Western Ghats region of the Deccan. These hill-men, largely an agrarian community, were sturdy and independent-minded and centuries of subjugation had made them wily. Many served as common soldiers in the army of the sultanate. The ancestors of Shivaji, the most revered hero of the Marathas, soldiered for the Sultan of Ahmadnagar. A forebear by the name of Shahji entered the Bijapur service and carved out "a vast estate for himself in the Mysore plateau and the eastern Karnatak and rose to be the foremost vassal of the Sultan of Bijapur".[258] His son, Shivaji, was born in 1627, in a hill village north of Poona.

Shivaji and Guru Hargobind were contemporaries. Both shared a common goal of a militarized people. Shivaji became the primal force for a sovereign Maratha state in the Deccan plateau, his homeland. Beginning in 1646 he captured the hill fort of Torna, garrisoned by Bijapur soldiers, located south-west of Poona about 40 Km away as the crow flies, making Marathas first among the indigenous peoples of the subcontinent of India to challenge foreign Muslim rule. By 1674, his dominion stretched over much of the mid-western region straddling the Sahyadri Mountain range (also known as Western Ghats) and

---

[258] The Mogul Empire by Ashirbadilal Srivastava –p.368

extending on to the Deccan plateau on the east (primarily southwestern region of present-day Maharashtra, sandwiched between Bombay in the North and Goa in the south).

With the passing of Aurengzeb in 1707, the Mogul empire entered an endless spiral of war of succession. This was nothing new as a culture of coveting the throne permeated strongly in all the heirs to the Mogul throne, infighting among whom was the rule and fratricide routinely practiced. What was different this time was the rapidity of the cascading of succession as evident from the fact that in the span of next fifty years ten different emperors were to occupy the Mogul throne.

The inheritors of the throne were a mere shadow of their predecessors known for charisma, strategic thinking, and political shrewdness. For example - Bahadur Shah (1707-1712) "popularly called a heedless king (Shah-be-khabar)"; Jahandar Shah (1712-1713) "spent his days in buffoonery and nights in drunken frolics"; Farrukh-Siyar (1713-1719) involved in "perpetual plotting" against his wazir; Muhammad Shah (1719-1748) "a weak and inexperienced prince"; and Ahmad Shah "dissipated, perfidious, pusillanimous and utterly worthless".[259]

The year Banda Bahadur irrupted into Malwa region of northern India in 1709, Shahu, Shivaji's grandson,

---

[259] The Mogul Empire by Ashirbadilal Srivastava – Chapter 10

was the undisputed overlord of the Marathas. In 1713, Shahu exalted Balaji Vishwanath, a staunch loyalist to the position of Peshwa (Prime Minister).[260] This did not sit well with Tara Bai. Since her husband, Shahu's uncle Raja Ram, was the one who had preserved the kingdom of the Marathas, she felt her son was the legitimate chhatrapati.[261] She saw her nephew Shahu as an imposter.[262]

---

[260] As Maratha overlord Sjhivaji had established a council of ministers (called Ashta Pradhan) and the senior most member of the council was designated Mukhya Pradhan or Peshwa (i.e. Prime Minister). He served as a deputy leader and was delegated effective control over entire administration including the armed forces.

[261] Meaning "overlord of the Maratha dominion"

[262] Shivaji died in April 1680 and survived by two sons. The elder named Sambhaji (b. 1686) was the issue of his first wife Sai Bai. His second wife Sorya Bai, his favourite, mothered the younger son, Raja Ram (b.1670). Shivaji left no clue about his successor, which caused Sorya, with the help of some influential Maratha chiefs, to install her son Raja Ram as chhatrapati. On hearing the news, Sambhaji, assisted by senapati (general) Hambir Rao Mohite stormed the Maratha capital Raigarh, enthroned himself chhatrapati and took into custody his stepbrother (Raja Ram) and step-mother (Sorya Bai). This event marked the beginning of war of succession.
In February 1689, Mogul commander took Sambhaji prisoner, and at the behest of Emperor Aurengzeb tortured to death. Maratha leaders freed Raja Ram from prison and invested him as Chhatrapati since Sambhaji's infant son, Shahu (b. 1682), widow Yesa Bai, and several Maratha sardars were state prisoners. Raja Ram died in 1700 of illness and, his son being a minor, his wife Tara Bai assumed regency. After Shahu's liberation, he ascended the throne in 1708. Tara Bai refused to acknowledge Shahu as she felt her son was the rightful inheritor

After defeating his cousin in 1731, Shahu dictated the Treaty of Warna by which the territories lying north of the Warna River belonged to Shahu and those south of the river ceded to Tara Bai's son Shambhaji. Thus the scions of Shivaji bifurcate Maratha kingdom in the Deccan plateau: Shahu ruled over the kingdom of Satara, and, his first cousin Shambhaji, ruled over the Kingdom of Kolhapur.

In the meantime, Mogul empire was losing its majesty and luster. The descent into atrophy accelerated on Farrukh-Siyar's ascension to the throne.[263] Farrukh-Siyar got embroiled with Sayyid brothers who had helped him secure the throne. Relations between the emperor and his wazir (Prime Minister) Abdullah Khan, one of the Sayyid brothers, turned so toxic that the latter appealed to his brother Husain Ali Khan, then the Governor of Deccan, for assistance. Determined to teach the emperor a lesson, Husain Ali Khan solicited a contingent of Maratha troops from Shahu and as a quid pro quo for his help offered Shahu governance of the six Mogul provinces of the Deccan as a vassal.

---

and it resulted in "civil war between the scions of Shivji's ruling house" – Shahu and Shivaji ll. The two rival factions fought it out at Khed, on the bank of Bhima Rvier, and Shhau prevailed. Tara Bai and her followers vacated Satara relocation to the south of Krishna River. Advanced Study in the History of Modern India 1707-1813 by Jaswant Lal Mehta – p46-63

[263] Farrukh-Siyar had a childish bent and was so incompetent that his wazir (Prime Minister) Sayyid Abdullah Khan became the de fact power behind the throne – The Mogul Empire by Ashirbadilal Srivastava p.416-417

In 1719, Farrukh-Siyar was overthrown and strangled. His nephew Rafi-ud-darajit, who ratified the treaty of assigning the Deccan provinces to Shahu, succeeded him in February. Within three months, Rafi-ud-darajit died of illness and succeeded by his elder brother Rafi-ud-daula, who assumed the title of Shah Jahan ll and died three months later of tuberculosis. His son Raushan Akhtar succeeded him and took the title of Muhammad Shah.[264]

On the death of Peshwa Balaji Vishwanath in 1720, Shahu confirmed his twenty-year-old son, Baji Rao, as Peshwa. Baji Rao correctly read the winds of change then blowing through imperial Mogul indicating an empire on the wane. He felt time was ripe "to drive the strangers from the country of the Hindus" and fly the Maratha flag from Krishna River (in present day Andhra Pradesh) to Attock (a city 80 Km north-west of Rawalpindi in present day Pakistan), a policy heartily endorsed by Shahu.[265]

---

[264] He was beholden to Sayyid brothers who customarily installed puppets of their own. Soon after his crowning, Muhammad Shah, in a strange turn of fate, had one Sayyid brother murdered and the other imprisoned. Court conspiracies began to abound and nobles jockeyed for plum jobs. Soon Muhammad Shah was locking horns in power battle with Nizam-ul-Mulk, the ruler of six subas in the Deccan. Nizam-ul-Mulk who was harried by the Marathas prevailed on them to leave him alone and instead focus on northern India (The Mogul Empire by Ashirbadilal Srivastava – p.420-423
[265] The Mogul Empire by Ashirbadilal Srivastava – p. 445

Consequently, in 1724, Baji Rao crossed Narmada River, a central Indian river running east to west that marks a natural line of demarcation between North and South India, and overran Malwa region of northern India (now part of Madhya Pradesh). Before he returned to Poona, Baji Rao installed Malhar Rao Holkar and Ranoji Scindia satraps and they in due time founded the princely states of Indore and Gwalior. In 1728, Shahu defeated the Mogul governor of Allahabad and wrested control of Bundelkhand.[266] In 1731, he secured Gujarat and appointed Pilaja Rao as governor (founder of Gaekwad dynasty of Baroda). In 1737, he crossed Jamna River and following his defeat of Nizam (Mogul proxy) at Bhopal, the emperor signed the treaty of Doraha Sarai under which sovereignty of territories between the Narmada and Chambal rivers ceded to the peshwa. On the passing of Baji Rao in 1740, Shahu appointed deceased's son Balaji as peshwa.[267]

The other unintended consequence of the weakened imperial power was the invasion of India, in 1738, by the Persian imperator, Nadir Shah, who was to defeat the Mogul forces at Karnal and then proceed to sack Delhi. The debilitation of the imperial rule by Nadir

---

[266] A territory now shared by Madhya Pradesh and Utter Pradesh
[267] Balaji was last of peshwas appointed by Shahu. The death of Shahu in December 1749 triggered an internecine feud among the descendants of Shivaji and despite the machinations of Tara Bai and Shahu's widow to preserve de facto authority of Chhatrapati (imperial title of Maratha ruler) all powers passed into the hands of the peshwas - The Mogul Empire by Ashirbadilal Srivastava – p. 456

Shah encouraged Maratha bands, led by Raghuji Bhonsle, to intensify their raids into west central India, Bengal, Bihar, and Orissa. An outraged Muhammad Shah appealed to Maratha peshwa (chief minister) Balaji Baji Rao to rein in the freelancing Maratha bands and as an affirmation of reliance appointed him governor of Malwa (circa 1738).

In 1741, Balaji Baji Rao marshaled his forces and headed for Bihar and Bengal. In 1743, he ousted Raghuji Bhonsle from Bihar, which was to promote an in-house imbroglio. Chatrapati (Lord of dominion) Shahu, Shivaji's grandson, ruler of Maratha kingdom, resolved the dispute by drawing a dividing line: central India remained under the aegis of Baji Rao and eastern India (Bengal, Orissa) awarded to Raghuji Bhonsle

In the mid-1740's Marathas got embroiled in the succession conflict to the throne of Jaipur that did not bode well for them. During same period, northern India became a happy hunting ground for the Afghan. The riches of India were the temptation for the Afghan leader Ahmad Shah Abdali to pillage the country.[268] His country of Afghanistan was poor

---

[268] This Indian treasure, which Abdali received as a windfall, enabled him to pay liberally other Afghan chiefs for their support and the soldiery to win their confidence. India was the treasure trove or an eldorado of Ahmad Shah Abdali, which he eagerly sought to possess. No wonder he proved to be the most formidable rival of the Marathas in the pursuit of their imperial

in resources and riven by factional conflicts and plots to usurp power. To hold onto power a suzerain, perforce, had to provide strong administration and maintain a standing army, and it was this economic imperative that led to the serial trampling across northern India by Abdali.

Aside from spoils, Abdali profited from his second invasion with the assignment of territories west of Indus River by the Mogul emperor as well as an annual tribute from four districts of Punjab. By terms of treaty signed in April 1752 following third invasion the Mogul emperor Ahmad Shah Bahadur ceded Lahore and Multan to Abdali. In early 1757, during his fourth invasion, Abdali sacked the imperial city of Delhi and before returning to Kabul bestowed Punjab upon his son, Taimur. The tightening of Afghan control over northern India effectively emasculated Mogul empire of Alamgir ll.

While Abdali was descending on Delhi from the north, Maratha general Raghunath Rao, younger brother of peshwa Balaji Baji Rao, left Poona in October 1756, advancing on the imperial capital from the south. In August 1757, the Maratha general captured Delhi and vast swathes of countryside up to Saharanpur and a stranglehold on the empire.[269]

---

aspirations in northern India – Advanced Study in the History of Modern India 1707-1813 by Jaswant Lal Mehta – p.249

[269] For example, in 1754 Ghazi-al-Din Khan, imperial wazir (Imad-al-Mulk) supported by Malhar Rao Holkar - peshwa's chief general in Malwa - laid siege to Delhi and compelled

The Maratha who had overpowering presence in the imperial city now had an eye on Punjab, a Mogul jewel, which was in the hands of Prince Taimur.[270] By 1758, the Marathas had grown so powerful that they irrupted into Punjab under the Maratha general Raghunath Rao. In April of same year the Marathas drove Taimur away, established a garrison and secured their rule over Lahore. Raghunath appointed Adina Beg Khan as the governor of Punjab[271]. On the passing of Adina Beg in September 1758 Sabaji Scindia succeeded him as governor of Punjab.

Smarting from expulsion from the imperial court, Najib-ud-Daula appealed to his patron Abdali for aid. Abdali needed little prodding as he was furious with

---

Emperor Ahmad Shah to dismiss his wazir Intizam-ud-Daula and appoint his nephew Imad-ul-Mulk as the prime minister. The latter then deposed Ahmad Shah and installed the second son of Jahandar Shah to the throne who reigned as Alamgir ll. Imad-ul-Mulk for the most part of his wazirship remained dependent on Maratha bayonets. Again, following his fourth invasion of India (1757) Abdali conferred title of Najib-ud-Daula on Ruhela tribal chief Najib Khan and entrusted him with protecting the emperor. This gesture directly challenged the authority of Imad-al-Mulk, and so riled him that he pleaded with Maratha peshwa Balaji Baji Rao for help. The allied forces besieged Najib in August 1757 and removed him from the imperial court - The Mogul Empire by Ashirbadilal Srivastava – p. 428-430

[270] After his fourth invasion Abdali returned to Kabul but assigned Punjab to his son Taimur and left the Prince with an army of ten thousand men under General Jahan Khan (A History of the Sikhs by Khushwant Singh – Vol. 1 p.145)u

[271] The Mogul Empire by Ashirbadilal Srivastava – p.431-432

rage about how the Marathas forced his son Taimur to vacate Lahore. Abdali mustered a large army, crossed the Indus in August 1759, and put Sabaji Scindia to flight. He then marched his army into Delhi and sent one of his divisions to intercept Maratha Chief Dattaji Scindia on his way towards Sirhind. In January 1760, the Afghans intercepted and defeated the Marathas at Barari Ghat, 16 Km north of Delhi.

The Maratha collapse at Barari Ghat prompted Maratha peshwa Balaji Baji Rao to muster an army under the command of his cousin Sadashiva Rao Bhau to repel the Afghan invader and re-establish Maratha suzerainty in northern India. While Abdali was encamped at Sikendrabad, he got wind of Bhau marching towards Sirhind, en route to Punjab. Abdalli rushed in pursuit of Bhau. Both armies faced one another at Panipat. They fought three battles and in the final clash in January 1761 the Maratha army suffered a catastrophic defeat, ending Maratha hegemony over Punjab. It also paved the way for the British entry into northern India.

Abdali's serial trespasses on northern India had made him all too aware of the rapidly disintegrating Mogul authority, which was his impulse to exploit the Mogul weakness and establish his authority. However, the emergence of Maratha power in northern India and the rise of Sikh misls in Punjab thwarted his dream of supplanting Mogul rule. Although he managed to crush the Marathas for the last time, his nemesis, the

Sikh misls, quashed his ambition of hegemony over Punjab.

INDIA 1705

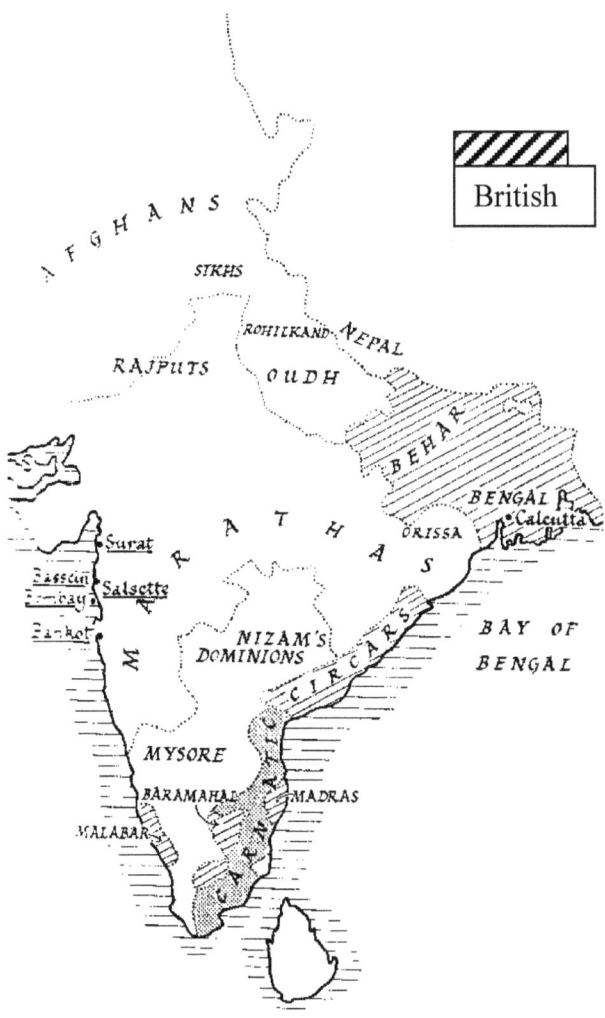

9. Emergence of Sikh hegemony over Punjab

The Moguls martyred Banda Bahadur in June 1716. The Sikh collectivity was now void of leadership. Some of his devoted followers, known as Bandais, turned to freelance banditry. However "many more bands of Sikh outlaws were operating in different parts of the province (Punjab)".[272]

These bands (Jathas) had carved Punjab into separate areas reflective of their individual strength and garrisoned themselves in mountain or jungle fastnesses. The modus operandi of these outlaws was very similar. They would swoop down on the plains to plunder zamindars and treasury-laden convoys.

To put a stop to the pillaging of the government treasuries, Zakaria Khan, Governor of Lahore, sent an envoy offering the Sikh bands a jagir (revenues from a district) and bestowing of the title Nawab (a high ranking designation). Persuaded to accept the Nawabship in 1733, Kapur Singh merged the various

---

[272] A History of the Sikhs by Khushwant Singh – Vol. 1 p.122 (footnote);
Between 1716 and 1726, these Sikh bands had "reorganized their forces and harassed the Mogul authorities from their hide-outs in the forests and the bushy wastes of the central tracts. Sometimes they would fall upon the Government treasury, at other times on the rich zemindars and other notables" (A History of the Sikh People by Dr. Gopal Singh p.364).

Jathas (bands) into an army consisting of two divisions: Buddha Dal and the Taruna Dal, and in 1748 fused these Jathas into one army, the Dal Khalsa.

In February 1739 Nadir Shah, ruler of Persia, invaded India and defeated the Mogul army at the Battle of Karnal, 110 Km north of Delhi. While homeward bound, laden with enormous booty, the Sikh Jathas (bands) ambushed him and plundered his train.

Nadir Shah's military forces included a Pashtun detachment, commanded by Ahmad Khan, a pious Muslim and a Sufi disciple. Following the murder of Nadir Shah in 1747, Ahmad Khan headed for Qandahar to consolidate his power in Afghanistan.[273]

---

[273] The death of Nadir Shah caused a great deal of turmoil in the Persian camp as Nadir Shah had ruled Iran and his troops with an iron fist and there was no generally accepted heir. Into this vacuum stepped a 25-year-old Ahmad Khan, son of the former ruler of Herat. He belonged to the Sardozay branch of the Popalzay tribe of the Abdali confederacy. After the conquest of Qandahar, Nadir Shah had sent Ahmad Khan to Mazandaran where the young Pashtun became a governor. At the time of Nadir Shah's death, he commanded a contingent of Abdali Pashtuns. Realizing that his life was in jeopardy among Persians who had murdered Nadir Shah, he left the Persian camp with 4,000 troops to Qandahar. Along the way and by sheer luck, they managed to capture a caravan with booty from India. He had no rights as to the control of the tribes themselves, apart from that of his own, Durrani group. The other tribes only followed him if he could provide them with booty. In 1747 he was crowned king and came to be known as Ahmad Shah Abdali (The Afghans by Willem Vogelsang – p.228-229)

Abdali was quick to realize his standing army that was the underpinning for his power would be in want of sustenance. He had seen firsthand the spoils carried away by Nadir Shah, including the famed Peacock throne. He began to entertain the idea of invading India. He also understood that many of the local chiefs would join him in his military adventurism in the expectation of plunder.

Before the advent of Abdali in India, Punjab was a prized province of the Mogul empire. The province prided itself of its diverse ethnic cultures, populated mainly by Mogul ruling class, Afghans, Muslim converts, Hindus and Sikhs. From time to time, the non-Muslim citizenry suffered discrimination in some form or the other (e.g. Jizya, a type of tax). Overall people lived side by side in harmony and went about their daily lives, as was their custom.

Mogul, the invader and occupier, gradually adapted to the customs and attitudes of the prevailing values and lifestyles and customs. Over time, the Moguls shed their native Turkic language, adopted Persian as the language of court, and phased it out in favour of Urdu, a hybrid language that borrowed grammar and vocabulary from several languages including indigenous ones.

There is no record of unrest or protest against the Mogul rule from any quarter. There is no credible evidence of an offensive by Banda Bahadur to topple the Mogul rule. He directed his campaign solely against those who had brutalized and tortured the Sikhs. Nationalism had not taken root.

Because of its unique geographical location, Punjab bore the brunt of invaders and, therefore, heavily garrisoned. Lahore was the Mogul capital of Punjab and Mogul nobles saw posting to Punjab as a privileged appointment. Moreover, the governorship of Lahore was the most coveted position to which appointments made on basis of nepotism and cronyism. Qamaruddin Khan, who served as the Chief Wazir to the Mogul emperor Muhammad Shah, appointed his nephew Zakaria Khan to govern Punjab (1726-1745).

Seat of secondary primacy power was the administrators of Jullundhar and Multan. In 1739 Zakaria Khan appointed Adina Beg Khan faujdar of Jullundhar; and, in 1747, Shah Nawaz appointed Kaura Mal, Diwan of Multan.[274] Of all the Mogul functionaries, Adina Beg was the most wiliest and Machiavellian, having no scruples in collaborating with even his enemies as long as it suited his interests.

The death of Zakaria Khan in 1745 triggered an internecine war of succession with the result that the governorship of Punjab alternated between his sons, Yahya Khan and Shah Nawaz, and his cousin Mir

---

[274] A History of the Sikhs by Khushwant Singh – Vol. 1 p.130

Mannu. From among them Mir Mannu emerged as the pivotal player. The inter-familial infighting provided the Sikh Jathas, hitherto hounded by Zakaria's police, the opportunity to recoup quietly their strength.[275]

Ahmad Shah Abdali invaded India for the first time in 1747. He reached Lahore in January 1748 and sacked the city. He advanced towards Delhi and at Mannupur some 20 Km northwest of Sirhind, he came face to face with the Mogul army led by Qamaruddin Khan. Qamaruddin died in battle while his son Mir Mannu put up a fierce battle and caused the Afghans to flee. The Sikh Jathas beset the retreating Afghans stealing their provisions and horses.

In the dead of winter of the same year (December 1748) Abdali set out on his second invasion. As he reached the western bank of the Chenab River, about 5 Km west of Wazirabad, he confronted Mir Mannu, the governor of Punjab, encamped on the eastern bank of the river. Abdali "hesitated to open hostilities with the man who had beaten him only nine months earlier" and in a tactical move sent a contingent of his army under the command of Jahan Khan to capture Lahore.

Mir Mannu's deputy mustered a force to intercept Jahan Khan. Simultaneously, the Sikhs led by Kapur

---

[275] A History of the Sikhs by Khushwant Singh – Vol. 1 p.130

Singh "swooped down on Lahore and for some hours had the pleasure of having the capital at their mercy". Mir Mannu made peace with Abdali and agreed to pay an annual tribute and, thus, "became a feudatory of the Afghan king".[276]

Abdali invaded Punjab for the third time in the autumn of 1751. Following year, near Lahore, he defeated the Mogul army led by Mir Mannu and Adina Beg that included a large contingent of Sikhs. In a treaty ratified by Mogul Emperor Ahmad Shah Bahadur in 1752, the emperor ceded Lahore and Multan to Abdali; and, thus Punjab fell under the suzerainty of the Afghans.

Some Sikh misldars took advantage of the unsettled conditions in the wake of the Mogul-Afghan battle by extending their domain from the river Ravi across the Sutlej all the way east to within fifty miles of Delhi. Still nursing his defeat at the hand of Abdali and incensed by the audacious expansion of Sikh into his territory, Mir Mannu mobilized his forces to search and destroy the roving Sikh bands.[277] For Adina Beg Khan who had lost most territory to the Sikhs, the situation was of greater urgency.

Both Mir Mannu and Adina Beg now hunted down the Sikhs. At first Adina Beg tried rapprochement with Jassa Singh Ahluwalia to resolve the territorial issue but to no avail. Instead, he was able to persuade

---

[276] A History of the Sikhs by Khushwant Singh – p. 135-136
[277] *Ibid.* – p.139-140

Jassa Singh Ramgarhia to join the Mogul forces that were to mount an attack on the Sikh fort of Ram Rauni. The Sikhs had dug a deep moat in defense of the fort. During the siege, the Sikhs "fell short of provisions" and forced out to engage the Mogul forces. This was the moment when Jassa Singh Ramgarhia walked over to the Sikh side, agreeing to do penance for the wrongs he had committed.[278]

The fighting and reprisals went on until Mir Mannu's death in November 1753. The governorship of Punjab became a cause of disagreement between Mogul Emperor Alamgir ll and Mir Mannu's widow and following an altercation between the two, the latter took over the administrative role. This in-house imbroglio, an acknowledgement of self-evident collapse of the administration of Punjab, did not escape the notice of the Sikh misldars who saw it as an opportunity to change their strategy: "instead of simply robbing the people" they "offered protection (rakhi)" on payment of one-fifth of their harvests.[279]

Abdali had "ruthlessly pillaged Delhi" during his fourth invasion. On returning to Lahore, he appointed his son, Prince Taimur, in 1756, as governor of Punjab. While homeward bound to Kabul, the Sikh bands set upon Abdali's booty laden caravan at several points. In retaliation he had Harminder Sahib "blown up and the scared pool filled with the entrails of slaughtered cows". To

---

[278] Sardar Jassa Singh Ahluwalia by Ganda Singh – p.59- p.60
[279] A History of the Sikhs by Khushwant Singh – p. 142

avenge the desecration of the holy temple Jassa Singh Ahluwalia with the help of ally Adina Beg defeated and vanquished the Afghan forces.[280]

Fearful of the rising power of the Sikhs that may jeopardize his own security, Adina Beg invited the Marathas to come to Punjab. In 1758 Maratha general, Raghunath Rao entered Punjab with a mighty army. Although now occupied nominally by the Moguls, Punjab was de facto in the hands of the Afghans and the Marathas, each power vying with the other to be the master of the land.[281]

Adina Beg's betrayal was unexpected and before the Sikhs could punish him, he died of colic in September 1758. In March 1759, Marathas occupied Lahore. Smarting from his prior year's defeat Abdali mustered a large army to crush the Marathas. This was Abdali's fifth invasion. The Afghans and the Marathas battled it out at Panipat in January 1761; Abdali decimated the Maratha army, thus ending Maratha imperialism of Punjab.

Abdali, war weary, turned homewards. Small Sikh Jathas would position themselves at strategic points on the route of his train and ambush the Afghans appropriating the spoils and rescuing Hindu women he had abducted. The repetitive guerilla attacks and

---

[280] History of the Sikhs by Khushwant Singh – p. 142 p.144 –p.145
[281] *ibid* – p.147- p.148

surprise ambushes by a small and highly mobile Sikh Jathas became a thorn in Abdali's flesh.

Abdali tasked his General Nur-ud-Din Bamzai to join forces with Obed Khan, the then governor of Punjab, to teach the Sikhs a lesson. En route to Lahore as Bamzai crossed Chenab with a 12,000 strong horse-cavalry he was to face an onslaught from Charat Singh Sukerchakia; routed, he fled to Sialkot with the Sikh misldar in hot pursuit. He made his escape and his army surrendered. Charat Singh Sukerchakia emerged from this crucible of guerilla warfare as an accomplished leader.[282]

The humiliating defeat of Bamzai so outraged Obed Khan that he dispatched a large force to attack the misldar's fort at Gujranwal. On hearing of the siege of the fort, Jassa Singh Ahluwalia accompanied by leaders of Bhangi and Kanhaya misls launched a counter attack, scattering the Mogul forces. Thus, Punjab, for the first time, came under Sikh orbit. The nobles of Lahore greeted the victorious Jassa Singh Ahluwalia as Sultan-ul-Qaum.[283]

Abdali tasked his General Noor-ud-Din Thamezai to take command of a 12,000 strong horse cavalry and lead an onslaught on the troublesome Sikhs. Charat Singh Sukerchakia confronted Thamezai, as he crossed Chenab, en route to Lahore. During fierce battle near Wazira Bagh, Thamezai retreated in

---

[282] A History of the Sikh People by Dr. Gopal Singh p.403
[283] *Ibid.* – p.404

disorder to a fort in Sialkot, with the Sikh misldar in hot pursuit. A besieged Thamezai managed to escape, and his army surrendered.[284]

This battle is noteworthy from the standpoint of a Sikh misldar inflicting a grievous blow to the seasoned Afghan warriors; and, from this triumph was to emerge Charat Singh Sukerchakia as a hero and an accomplished leader.[285]

Ubed Khan, the then governor of Punjab, saw Thamezai's humiliating rout as an embarrassment to Mogul power and was beside himself with rage. He marched with a large army to launch an attack on Gujranwala, the stronghold of Sukerchakia misl. Word of the impending attack reached Jassa Singh Ahluwalia who along with the Kanhaya and Bhangi misldars came to the aid of Charat Singh Sukerchakia. Their combined forces threw the enemy into disarray and as they fled the field, they left behind vital war assets, which included artillery. The Sikh forces chased and encircled Ubed Khan in the Lahore fort. However, the nobles of Lahore realized that Ubed Khan was a spent force, opened the city gates, and greeted the victorious Jassa Singh Ahluwalia as Sultan-ul-Qaum (November 1761).[286] Within a few weeks, the Sikhs had "the entire province from the Sutlej to the Indus under their control".[287]

---

[284] Sardar Jassa Singh Ahluwalia by Ganda Singh – p.107 – p.108
[285] A History of the Sikh People by Dr. Gopal Singh p.403
[286] *Ibid.* – p.404
[287] A History of the Sikhs by Khushwant Singh – Vol. 1 p.153

Overrunning of Lahore by his nemesis, the Sikhs, while governor Ubed Khan remained ensconced in the Lahore fort, so incensed Abdali that he immediately marched into Punjab for the sixth time. Abdali reoccupied Lahore and set out on the trail of the retreating Sikhs. The subsequent encounter with the Sikhs at the village of Kup (February 1762) was to culminate in the massacre of thousands of Sikh men, women and children (Vada Ghallughara); and, later, with the desecration of Harminder Sahib yet again.

In December 1762, Abdali appointed Kabuli Mal as governor of Lahore and left Lahore for Kabul. This was the signal for the Sikh misldars to start moving from their hideouts to reoccupy the territories that were part of their sphere of control and to reconstruct the demolished Harminder Sahib.

While celebrating Baisakhi 1763 in Amritsar, a Brahmin from Kasur pleaded with the misldars to rescue his wife from Usman Khan Kasuria. The misldars led by Hari Singh of Bhangi misl and Charat Singh of Sukerchakia misl marched to Kasur and after a brief encounter liberated the kidnapped woman. They then plundered the rich city. The offensive carried into sacking of Malerkotla, killing of its nawab, followed by an attack on Sirhind and slaying of its Afghan administrator, Zain Khan.

The account of Sikh aggression reached Abdali in November 1763. He at once dispatched his General Jahan Khan to punish the Sikhs. As soon as Charat

Singh Sukerchakia heard the news that the General had crossed Chenab River en route to Sialkot, he sent word to fellow misldar chieftains for help. Both Jassa Singh Ahluwalia and the sardars of Bhangi misl enlisted to help. The combined forces of Sikh misldars clobbered the Afghans who fled the field, as did Jahan Khan. They now occupied the entire territory between Jhelum and the Indus River and divided it between the Sukerchakia misl and the Bhangi misl.

Abdali was angry and humiliated that his Afghan proxies had been badly defeated. He invited Nasir Khan, the Baluch ruler, to ally with him in a jihad against the Sikhs; thus, began Abdali's seventh invasion. Kabuli Mal, the governor of Lahore, greeted them warmly. The Afghan armies then marched towards Amritsar. Though harried by guerilla tactics of the Sikh Jathas the Afghans massacred villagers and devastated the countryside. This rampage stoked the wrath of the leading Sikh misldars (Bhangi, Sukerchakia, Kanhaya, Ramgarhia, and Ahluwalia) who waylaid Abdali while he was returning to Kabul.

A few days after Abdali's exit from Punjab, Sarbat Khalsa met in April 1765 and resolved to retake Lahore. When the combined forces of Bhangi and Kanhaya misls captured Lahore, the local citizenry implored misldars to spare the city ordeal of plunder, as the city was Guru's cradle (being the birthplace of Ram Das, the fourth Guru). The misldars divided the city between them: Bhangi sardar Lehna Singh occupying the central part that included the fort; Bhangi sardar Gujjar Singh the eastern parts; and, the Kanhaya sardar Sobha Singh the southern part.[288]

In November 1766, Abdali entered Punjab for the eighth time "to utterly devastate a land which gave birth to and sheltered these reckless infidels (Sikhs)".[289] This triggered another seesaw movement forcing the misldars occupying Lahore to vacate the city. In January 1767, Abdali General Jahan Khan decided to march to Amritsar and met by a combined force of misldars who killed thousands of Afghans. Abdali came to the rescue of his beleaguered general but this time did not desecrate the temple.

Abdali continued his march crossing the Sutlej into Malwa where the Rohilla chief Najibuddaulah and Phulkian chief Amar Singh joined him. The district of Sirhind that Abdali had in 1764 bestowed upon Ala Singh, now he was to award it to Ala's grandson Amar Singh for his loyalty to the Afghan invader.

Abdali turned around homeward bound and as he crossed the Indus, the three misldars returned to reoccupy Lahore. By the end of the year, Punjab became the domain of the Sikh misls.

In 1769, Abdali marched into Punjab for the ninth time but did not advance beyond Jhelum River in what was an expedition rather than an invasion. He

---

[288] A History of the Sikhs by Khushwant Singh – p.160 –p.161
[289] A History of the Sikh People by Dr. Gopal Singh p.411

was a sick man, afflicted with a painful cancer of the nose ever since 1764. By now he had had lost his conquistador edge, was a shadow of his former self, an aging warrior, tired and unsure of himself. He returned to Kandhar and died three years later in October 1772.

Abdali invaded India nine times. His intent was not one of conquest and rule. Punjab was to be his vassalage governed through a proxy. Loot and plunder was his main preoccupation. However, his quest for and accumulation of riches was thwarted by repeated ambushes by armed Sikh Jathas who in turn robbed him.

Abdali, therefore, was bitterly against the Sikhs and obsessed to rid Punjab of Sikh presence. The misldars were equally determined to rid Punjab of Afghan dominance. Both parties saw Lahore as the key to governance of Punjab. During the decade following the installing of Kabuli Mal as governor of Punjab until his death in 1772 Abdali and the Sikh misldars locked horns in a deathly dance.

His son Taimur Shah who left no mark on the Punjab theatre succeeded Abdali. On his death in 1793, his son Shah Zaman assumed the mantle of authority and like his grandfather Abdali, he, too, nursed no less zeal to regain a foothold in north India.

To assuage his hankering Shah Zaman made three forays into Punjab (November 1795, December 1796 and October 1797), the first time at the invitation from Mogul emperor Shah Alam ll who wished to rid of Maratha control over him. The first two invasions ended in a stalemate and he had to make a hasty retreat to Kabul to put down an insurrection by his brother at Herat. He intended his last incursion in 1791 to punish the Sikh misldars for inflicting heavy losses he suffered from their ambushes in prior two invasions.

During the same period, misldars were engaged in an increasingly fractious relationship. This became quite obvious as Cis-Sutlej states (Latin Cis meaning: "this side of") situated south of river Sutlej, consisting principally of Patiala, Faridkot, Jind and Nabha, would willingly accept being Afghan's tributary while some other misldars offered safe passage in return for shared booty. For example, during the second invasion Shah Zaman received obeisance (arzi) from Sahib Singh chief of Phulkian misl.

Disunity compounded the difficulties of head-on military confrontation with the Afghan invaders. Ordinarily, on hearing that the Afghan ruler Abdali, later Shah Zaman, was on his usual rampage through Punjab, Sikh misldars would vacate their occupied territories and scamper off to their hideouts. They would lie in wait for a homeward bound Abdali, laden with heavy booty, then descend on the plains, ambush and loot him and flee to their strongholds in the hills. These were the customary cat-and-mouse tactics of the misldars.

Things were no different in the winter of 1797 when Sikh misldars learned of Afghan ruler Shah Zaman's march into Punjab. Immediately the misldars sent their families to safe havens and made their way to Amritsar in time for Diwali celebrations. Sahib Singh, chief of Phulkian misl, was the only hold out. Those assembled harboured suspicious of one another.

Ranjit Singh of Sukerchakia misl pleaded with fellow misldars for a unified alliance against the Afghan. The story goes that Sada Kaur, Ranjit's mother-in-law, now also leader of Kanhaya misl, scornfully remarked to the assembled misldars that if they were not men enough to resist the Afghan then "change your dress with me and I will proceed against the enemy".[290] Thus, the six of the misldars ally themselves with Ranjit Singh of Sukerchakia misl and Sada Kaur's Kanhaya misl.

The united misl front moved towards Lahore. They fought several battles with various Afghan detachments inflicting serious losses. Shah Zaman sued for peace and aware of the discord between the misldars schemed to divide them further by bribing individual misldars with promises of a jagir (barony). Even Ranjit Singh sent his intermediary to "negotiate the subedari of Lahore in order to offset the moves of other sardars".[291]

---

[290] A History of the Sikh People by Dr. Gopal Singh p.437
[291] A History of the Sikhs by Khushwant Singh – Vol. 1 p.194-p.195

Sahib Singh Bedi, a descendant of Guru Nanak, speaking on behalf of all misldars cautioned Shah Zaman that "we took the country by the sword and we will preserve it by the sword", and thus saved the situation.[292]

News of revolt by his half brother Mahmud backed by Barakzai warrior, Fateh Khan, forced Zaman Shah to repair to Kabul posthaste. Sensing the propitious omen in the unfolding events, Sahib Singh Bedi smeared Ranjit Singh's forehead with a saffron tilak and proclaimed him Maharaja of Punjab.[293]

---

[292] A History of the Sikhs by Khushwant Singh – Vol. 1 – p.195
[293] *ibid* – p.200

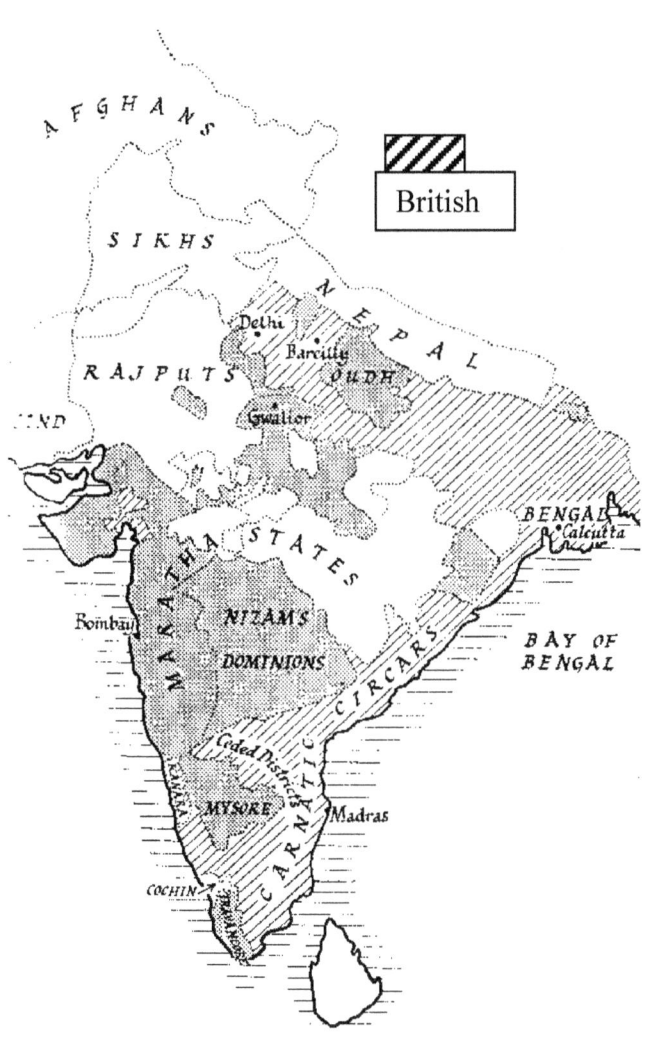

INDIA 1805

9. EPILOGUE

As happens to legends in all cultures, stories about misls over time became gilded and romanticized. Sentimentalists have spun fanciful tales of accomplishments of misls. That misls exuded nationalism, laid the cornerstone of nation state, and were the precursor of the Sikh kingdom is a popular perception. Hence, the word misl has become an irresistible metaphor for Sikh empowerment.

The hard cold facts of history tell a different story. Self-ennoblement was the primary raison d'etre of the misldars. They had no hankering to mount a revolt against the Mogul rule or to rid Punjab of Abdali, the Afghan scourge. They showed no desire to occupy space or territory to establish a Sikh state. At least not until the chieftain of Sukerchakia took upon himself the task to do so.

When the Sikhs established their confederacy on Baisakhi day 1748, Punjab was a Mogul province. At the time sovereignty, the world over, rested in the hands of monarchs, emperors, or sultans who ruled over multi-ethnic populations and the idea of rule by consent of the people was not yet on the horizon.[294]

---

[294] Europe was ruled by monarchs: Louis XV (France); George ll (Britain); Frederick ll (Prussia); Asia-Pacific by Emperors: Qing dynasty (China); Momozono (Japan); Elizabeth Petrtovna (tsarina Russia); Asia by Sultans: Mahmud l (Ottoman Turkey); Shahrukh Afshar (Persia); Ahmad Shah Abdali (Afghanistan),

Before the Muslim invasions, the political geography of northwestern sector of the Indian subcontinent was extremely fluid; borders were not just porous but shifted depending on the adventurer or conqueror. People moved about freely, and villages peopled by diverse cultures (Muslim, Afghan, Rajput, Hindu, and Punjabi tribes). For example, the sovereignty of Jaipal, the Rajput ruler of Punjab, extended to Laghman, a territory mostly populated by Muslims, lying west of the Indus River, now part of Afghanistan.[295]

The first Muslim to invade Punjab was Sabuktagin, ruler of Ghazni, who was Turkish by birth. In 977 A.D., he vanquished Jaipal and returned to Ghazni laden with large booty. After his death, Mahmud, his eldest son succeeded him. Mahmud greatly extended his empire by subduing neighbouring fiefdoms and in time honoured as Sultan of Ghaznavi. Mahmud pillaged northern India umpteen times. He levied tribute on defeated foes (petty Rajput princes) and embedded satrap in Multan.

When Mahmud died in 1030, his son Masud inherited the Sultanate. He rampaged through all the way to Sonipat (Circa 1036) and installed his son Maudud as

---

Ahmad Shah Bahadur (Mogul India). One privileged ethnic group dominated the empire and the population was largely culturally diverse. French and the American revolutions were in the distant future.

[295] Laghman is one of the provinces of Afghanistan bounded by administrative units Kabul on the west, Konar on the east and Nangarha in the south and Badakhshan in the north.

governor of Lahore. Lahore lies at the heart of Punjab, a city in the field of vision of conquerors. In 1043, confederacy of Hindu rajas made the first attempt to recover Lahore but to no avail.[296]

Successive Afghan rulers continued their onslaughts on northern India, of whom Ahmad Shah Abadli (c.1722-1773) left the largest footprint. He first invaded northern India in 1747 and his last and ninth invasion was in 1769. It was during these invasions of Ahmad Shah Abadli that the Sikhs came to assert their presence in Punjab.

Until they lost reins of power, Moguls were the only polity known to India.[297] The sun was starting to set

---

[296] History of the Punjab by Syed Muhammad Latif published 1891- p.87-88

[297] During the three millennia before the Mughul period (1526-1739), there was no single Indian polity congruent with Indian civilization. The so-called empires that commence with the Mauryans in 321 BC were loosely articulated, short-lived, and few. Briefly speaking, if we add the span of effective unity under the Mauryan, Gupta, and Delhi dynasties it amounts in total to little more than 362 years, demonstrating dramatically that on the Indian subcontinent empire was very much the exception and transience the norm. ….they represent a wholly unoriginal form of polity for, leaving aside the scatter of tribal oligarchies whose life span was in any case comparatively short, the norm was autocratic, even despotic, monarchy……the fact is that until the Mughul times India was simply a geographic expression.
It was not like the mono-cultural and for the most part politically united China. Studying it is more like studying Europe, with its diverse languages, religions, and peoples, and its many states which, like those of India, were continually at war……Until the

upon the Mogul empire from the dawn of the eighteenth century as the empire found it battling with the Afghan and Maratha aspirants to the hegemony over Punjab. Much of the time, northern India was, therefore, in a constant state of flux. In this crucible of turbulence, the Sikh misls were to forge their future. Thus, beginning in 1748, the Sikhs began to assert aggressively their presence in Punjab.[298]

First, there were tensions within the peasantry that needed to be lessened or resolved. For example, during the time of the Gurus, many peasants of Punjab, including Jats, soldiered for the imperial army because the Moguls regarded highly their indomitable spirit, and fighting skills. Some were hired mercenaries employed by local zamindars or mercantile community. Such secured tenure provided a decent standard of living not otherwise achievable with peasant farming. However, the advent of the

---

Mughuls, then, the efforts at political unification of the subcontinent were few, short lived, and territorially wanting. By contrast Mughul Empire was longer-lived and, at its height, embraced more territory than Ashoka's......a truly unitary state held together by (for its time) a sophisticated administration – (The History of Government Vol lll Empires, Monarchies and the Modern State by S.E. Finer; Chapter 4 pages 1210-1214)

[298] Baisakhi 1748 witnessed the merging of the independent Sikh jathas (bands) into one army, Dal Khalsa, consisting of eleven misls. Dal Khalsa met biannually at Amritsar at gatherings called as Sarbat Khalsa. In 1802, Ranjit Singh wrested Amritsar, the second most important city of Punjab, from the Bhangis and thereby establish his suzerainty over Punjab. According to Dr. Gopal Singh the leader of Dal Khalas was head of both the state (temporal) and church (spiritual).

Khalsa fostered a culture of dharamyudh i.e. war against oppression and in defense of righteousness. "The salaried soldier or commander was a nauker, a hired servant, expected to be loyal to his master, and the Khalsa Sikhs viewed this service, particularly service to the Mughals, as contemptible. A hired soldier fought for personal profit (whereas) the Khalsa soldier was expected to fight in defense of his fellow Sikhs and for the glory of the faith".[299]

The Sikh misldars promoted the Khlasa creed with the result that Sikh peasants vacated their service to imperial agencies and threw their lot with their community and faith. The peasants abandoning imperial service formed a large pool of military recruitment for the misldars. The chiefs with larger treasury and capacity to accumulated wealth through pillage gained the most recruits.

There is no record in the chronicles of Sikh confederacy attesting to Sikh misls, severally or as confederates, engaging in battle with Abdali face-to-face.[300] During Abdali's nine invasions, between 1747

---

[299] When Sparrows Became Hawks: The Making of the Sikh Warrior Tradition 1699-1799 by Purniman Dhavan page 75

[300] An exception may be battle of Mahilpur, in the district of Hoshiarpur, in December 1757. This battle, however, was to avenge the desecration of Harminder Sahib by Taimur's general Jahan Khan. But in this battle Dal Khalsa supremo Jassa Singh Ahluwalia, formed an alliance with Adina Beg, Taimur Shah's appointee to the post of commander of Jullundur, and routed the Afghans.

and 1769, the general modus operandi of the misldars was to play cat and mouse with Abdali. On hearing of Abdali marching into Punjab, misldars would vacate their headquarters in the plains and flee to their sanctuaries in the hills and jungles. Only the moment Abdali turned homeward bound laden with spoils they harried the raider and robbed him of his booty at many points.

Abdali's invasions took their toll on the Mogul emperors and their grip on Punjab began to slip away, which, in turn, resulted in the Lahore governor hamstrung by not being able to obtain support from Delhi. This opened the door for the misldars who stepped into the political vacuum and they began to sweep into their realm villages in the territories in the three doabs (Rechna, Bari, and Bist). These losses of imperial domain often got the misldars in the crosshairs of Mogul rulers and the two adversaries caught in several skirmishes in which one side or the other temporarily prevailed.

During the same epoch, misldars were hell-bent on capturing Lahore. However, Lahore, the most prized city and one that held the key to governance of Punjab, still eluded them. The city governed by a

---

Taimur sent another contingent of twenty thousand from Lahore to restore status quo, which in turn were defeated. But Adina Beg was becoming apprehensive of the rising power of the Sikhs and being a chameleon invited Marathas to come to Punjab (Sardar Jassa Singh Ahluwalia by Ganda Singh – Chapter 14)

Mogul or Afghan proxy remained heavily garrisoned.[301] As the misldars got stronger, they got bolder. They made frequent forays against the Muslim governor until the triad of Bhangi sardars (Lehna Singh, Gujjar Singh and Sobha Singh) captured the city.

That self- aggrandizement was the impulse of the misldars is an inescapoable conclusion. They took villages under their protection to empower themselves. They fought one another over land. They joined forces with the enemy to cut other misldars down to size. Nowhere is evidence of the misldars, severally or in collaboration, attempting to dislodge the Mogul or Afghan ruler of Punjab to establish Sikh supremacy. Rather the Marathas showed their true mettle by wanting to rid Punjab of the serial Afghan invader Abdali.

There is no evidence indicating that the Sukerchakia chief, Ranjit Singh, made it his mission to free Punjab from the clutches of Afghan and Mogul rulers and turn Punjab into a viable Sikh state. He believed in incremental inroads and seized real estate that he could hold and protect. From the beginning, he coveted Lahore, which he would have failed to capture, were it not for the help of the Kanhaya leader Sada Kaur who mounted the assault on the Delhi gate. Once he held dominion over Majha and

---

[301] Governors of Lahore: Shah Nawaz (1747); Mir Manu (1748) his infant son (1753) and widow (1754); Taimur (1757), Adina Beg (1758); Kabuli Mal (1765)

Doaba regions, he had visions of extending Sikh rule east of Sutlej River into the Malwa region. As noted before, his dream for greater Punjab shattered because of the perfidy of the Malwa sardars, principally Phulkian misldar, who chose to become British vassals.

GLOSSARY

Akal Takh	The principal Takht located adjacent to Haminder Sahib (Golden Temple)
Amrit	Sweetened initiation water used in baptism
Amritdhari	A baptized Sikh and an initiated member of the Khalsa
Asa Di Var	Selected hymns from the sacred scriptures recited in early hours of morning
Bachitra Natak	(Resplendent drama) A composition by Guru Gobind Singh
Bairagi	A religious mendicant
Baisakhi	Beginning of solar year in Punjab, the first day of the month of Baisakh
Bandai	Name given to followers of Banda Bahadur who regarded him their military and spiritual leader
Bigha	In Punjab 1 bigha = one-sixth of an acre
Buddha Dal	One of two militia groups within Dal Khalsa
Chaudhary	A title awarded by Mogul emperors conferring ancestral ownership of land
Dal Khalsa	An organization comprising two militia groups (Buddha Dal and Taruna Dal)

Damdama Sahib	One of five Takhts (seat of temporal power), meaning 'breathing space'
Darbar	A court or audience chamber
Dharamyudh	A war in defence of righteousness
Diwan	Regional governor
Doab	A tract of land between two confluent rivers
Faujdar	A garrison commander
Firman	A royal decree or order
Ghallughara	holocaust or carnage
Gurmatta	holy resolution affecting principles of Sikh faith
Guru Granth	the holy book of the Sikhs
Harminder Sahib	The Golden Temple located in Amritsar built by the fifth Guru
Hukamnama	Command or request issued by one of the Gurus to an individual or congregation; and, a similar document issued to the Sikh collectivity by Jathedar of Akal Takht
Jagir	A grant of public revenues of a district
Jatha	An armed gang
Jathedar	Commander of a Jatha; modern day chief officer of one of the five Takhts
Khalsa	The religious order established by Guru Gobind Singh
Kirtan	Singing of hymns
Kotwal	Chief constable

Masand	Functionaries organizing worships and collect offerings on behalf of the Guru
Miri	Temporal power
Misl	A warrior band
Misldar	Leader of the warrior band
Mouzas	A land area consisting of one or more settlements
Nagara	A war drum
Nauker	A hired servant
Nawab	A title bestowed by Mogul emperor to partially self-governing Muslim rulers
Panj Piyare	Literally "five beloved ones"; a name given to five baptized Sikhs
Panth	Sikh collectivity
Pargana	A revenue unit consisting of several villages
Peshwa	Maratha title equivalent to modern day Prime Minister
Pir	Head of a religious group; a tile given to Sufi masters
Piri	Spiritual power
Qazi	A judge whose decisions are based on Islamic religious laws
Rakhi	Buying of 'protection' of limb and property
Sansi	A nomadic tribe
Sant Siphai	Saint soldier
Sarbat Khalsa	A deliberative assembly of Sikh community
Sardar	A military or political leader

Sarkar	A district
Subedar	Governor of a province
Taruna Dal	One of two militia groups within Dal Khalsa
Wazir	A high ranking political advisor or minister
Zamindar	A land owner

INDEX

Abdul Samad Khan
tasked by Mogul emperor to punish Banda, 58
captures Banda and followers and takes them to Delhi, 59

Adina Beg
lay siege of Ram Rauni, 104
persuades Ramgarhia chief to mount attack on Amritsar, 104
appointed governor of Punjab by Marathas, 184
invites Marathas to come to Punjab, 195

Ahluwalia, 74, 76, 79, 88, 90, 92, 105, 107, 113, 124, 126, 129, 131, 134, 135, 159, 163, 166, 167, 194, 195, 196, 199
help Kanhaya in expelling Ramgarhias from Bist-Doab, 98
Jassa Singh taken into custody by Ramgarhias, 107
bloodline to Bhatti Rajputs mingled with Jats, 126
name derived from village Ahlu founded by Sadhu Singh, 126
birth of Jassa Singh, Taken to Delhi to meet Mata Sundri, 127
Jassa Singh acknowledged religious leader, 130
chose Kaputhala as headquarters, 131

Ahmad Shah Abdali, 12, 75, 81, 87, 104, 135, 141, 182
ousts Sabaji Scindia from Punjab, 185
campaign to teach the Sikhs a lesson, 196
a shadow of his former self, 201
left largest foot print in Punjab, 209

Akbar
establishes hierarchical system of government, 16
death set in a train of disasters, 19
dies October 1605, 19

Ala Singh
greatly extended his realm, 133
Phul's grandson, 133
victor over Rajput and Pathan
bestowed title of raja, 133
did not come to the aid of beseiged families - Vadda Ghallughara, 134

provides sycophantic
  succor to Abdali, 135
Abdali awards Sirhind for
  loyalty, 201
Anandpur Sahib
  Guru Gobind Singh
    evacuates city never to
    return, 39
  Hill chiefs and Mogul
    forces lay siege to the
    city, 39
Aurengzeb, 29, 34, 38, 43, 44, 177
  war of succession, 26
  preoccupied in Deccan
    territories, 34
Baba Deep Singh
  custodian of Damdama
    Sahib, 122
  founded Shaheedan misl,
    122
Babar
  marches upon Delhi, 84
Badar Singh
  baptized by Kapur Singh,
    127
  begets a son named Jassa
    Singh Ahluwalia, 127
Baghel Singh
  Karorasinghian misldar,
    116
  in alliance with other
    misldars sacks towns
    and unhinges Mogul
    emperor, 117
  Karorasinghian chief builds
    gurdwaras
    Bangla Sahib, Sis Ganj
    and Rakab Ganj,
    118

all his possessions were
  located in Cis-Sutlej,
  119
Bahadur Shah
  succession to the Mogul
    throne, 44
  mobilizes forces against
    the Sikhs, 55
Banda Bahadur, 47, 49, 54, 55, 57, 59, 61, 64, 66, 68, 69, 72, 81, 86, 103, 112, 122, 177, 187, 190
  initiation into Khalsa, 47
  entrusted as military
    commander, 47
  warmly received in Delhi,
    49
  establishes presence in
    Malwa region, 55
  rampage through Samana,
    57
  creates spiritual ministry,
    61
  changes religious
    institutions and laws, 65
  portrayed as brave but
    cruel, 66
  claim wrested extensive
    territories in dispute, 68
  redeems himself, 70
  followers not just
    leaderless but penniless
    called themselves
    Bandais, 71
  taken prisoner 1715, 59
  whereabouts from 1712 to
    1715 a mystery, 62
Battles
  battle of Achal 1783, 5

battle of Bhangani, 33
battle of Nadaun, 34
battle of Jajau 1707, 44
Dal Khalsa attack Patiala in 1764, 88
battle of Jammu 1774, 89
battle of Dina Nagar, 90
battle of Kot Kamalia, 121
battle of Goharwal, 122
battle of Zahura 1775, 129
battle of Panipat 1761, 141
battle of Ferozshah, 142
inter-misl battle of Batala, 152
inter-misl battle of Bhasin, 165
battle of Karnal, Nadir Shah defeats Moguls, 188
battle of Wazira Bagh, Sukerchakia attack Afghans, 197

Bhag Singh
a brigand of note, 126
seeks custody of young Jassa Singh Ahluwalia, 128
takes over command following demise of Jassa Singh 130

Bhai Mani Singh
asked to end factionalism, 73

Bhangi, 77, 79, 83, 86, 87, 89, 91, 94, 96, 107, 115, 124, 148, 150, 153, 157, 158, 164, 166, 196, 197, 199, 213

strength at 20,000 horsemen, 83
founded by Chhaja Singh, 86
Gurbaksh Singh joins the misl, 86
controlled greatest territorial range, 87
Hari Singh takes over leadership, 87
how name derived, 87
turns into an alliance of three leading sardars, 88
Ganda Singh succeeds Jhanda Singh
seekd vengeance against Kanhaya misldar, 89
in alliance with Ramgarhia chief engage with Kanhaya and Sukerchakia forces at Dina nagar, 90
leadership devolves on minor Desa Singh prompts infighting, 90
sibling infighting a despondent Gujjar Singh, 92
three misldars occupying Lahore under attack from Ranjit Singh and Sada kaur in 1799 95
Ranjit Singh captures Lahore, 96, 157
face Ranjit Singh at the battle at Bhasin, 96
disintegration of the once mighty misl, 96
sibling quarrels lead to fratricide, 164

Bhim Singh, 86, 87

Charat Singh
  forms Sukerchakia misl, 147
  succeeds Nodh Singh, decides to breakway from Fyzulpuria misl, 147
  marries daugther of Amir Singh of Gujranwala
  Charat and Amir formed own band named Sukerchakia, 147
  sacked Eminabad and Wazirabad
  envy of rival misldars, 148
  killed during encounter with Bhangi misl, 149
Chet Singh, 94
Chhaja Singh, 86
Dal Khalsa
  attack Patiala in 1764, 88
  outraged that Ala Singh sided with Abdali, 88
  Supreme commander Jassa Singh Ahluwalia mounts attack against Nijab-ul-Daula, 115
  declare war on Phulkian misl, 135
Dallewalian
  aligned with other Malwa based misldars to confront rivals, 120
  founded by Ghulab Singh, 120
Dasaunda Singh
  founded Nishanwalia misl, 123
  died in action against Nijab-ul-Daula, 124
Desa Singh, 90, 150
Fateh Singh (Ahluwalia), 92
  Ordered to divest Budh Singh of his possessions, 114
  exchanges turban with Ranjit Singh, 131
Fateh Singh (Bhangi), 93
  seeks title to lost estates, 93
Ganda Singh, 88, 89, 92, 107
Ghallughara
  massacre of Sikhs (1746), 75
Gujjar Singh, 86, 87, 90, 91, 93, 153, 164, 200
Gulab Singh, 91, 96
  extends domain around Amritsar, 91
Gurbaksh Singh, 5, 86, 88, 99, 105, 118, 124, 152, 164, See Bhangi
  adopts Lehna Singh as son, 88
Guru Arjun Dev
  charged for treason, 19
  charged with treason, 19
Guru Gobind Singh

relocation to Paonta Sahib, 30
suspicions of Hill chiefs, 32
confront Mogul forces at Nadaun, 34
return to Anandpur Sahib, 34
composes Bachitra Natak, 35
summons to Sikhs to descend on Anandpur Sahib on Baisakhi 1699, 35
evacuates Anandpur Sahib, 39
seek refuge in Chamkaur, 40
martyrdom of 40 Sikhs, 42
sacrifice of Guru's two sons, 41
founding of the Khalsa, 36
imperative to go to the Deccan, 43
travel to Talwandi Sabo, 43
notion of warrior saint, 45
assassination, 45

Guru Har Rai
ostracizes elder son, 26
show of empathy for Dara Shikoh, 26

Guru Hargobind
promotes notion of miri and piri, 20
builds Akal Takht, 21
establishes military training camps, 21
imbues his followers with military zeal, 21
right to defend the faith, 23
warrant for arrest, 23
clashes with Moguls, 25
anoints grandson as successor, 25
battle of Bhangani, 32
beginnings of armed panth, 51

Guru Tegh Bahadur
Founding of Anandpur Sahib, 27
Champion of human rights, 28
Pandits seek help, 28
put to death, 30

Hardas Singh
has grandson named Jassa Singh (Ramgarhia), 103

Hari Singh, 73, 87, 90, 199

Hemu
captures Delhi
enthroned emperor, 174

Hira Singh
founded Nakkai misl, 120
mounts attack on Pakpattan, 121

India
known by name Hindustan, 13

Jai Singh, 74, 89, 94, 98, 99, 105, 107, 149, 152, 155, 163, 167
baptized by Kapur Singh, 97
Chief of Kanhaya misl, 97
mentor to Maha Singh a Sukerchakia scion, 98

Jala-ud-Din

executioner of Guru Tegh
   Bahadur, 57
**Jaspat Rai, Faujdar of
   Emnabad, 74**
**Jassa Singh Ahluwalia,
   76, 88, 107, 113,
   115, 124, 130, 134,
   136, 194, 196, 198**
   made ward of Kapur
      Singh, 127
   separates from Kapur
      Singh
   forms his own band,
      129
   succeeded by cousin Bhag
      Singh, 130
**Jassa Singh Ramgarhia,
   90, 91, 96, 98, 103,
   106, 109, 129, 152,
   158, 165, 194**
   declared persona non grata,
      103
   agrees to do penance for
      his wrongs, 194
Jathas
   independent, own leader,
      own flag, 74
   harried and looted Abdali's
      baggage, 76
   members preferred pillage
      over sustenance
      farming, 82
   pillagers turned protectors
      (rakhi), 83
Jats
   sturdiest peasants, 52
   impulse to throw off the
      yoke of Mogul rule, 53

**Jhanda Singh, 89, 92,
   97, 107, 148**
   marches upon Jammu and
      is assassinated, 89
Jodh Singh
   takes over Karorasinghian
      misl leadership, 119
**Kanhaya, 74, 77, 79,
   89, 90, 94, 96, 97,
   99, 101, 105, 108,
   109, 115, 124, 139,
   149, 151, 154, 163,
   165, 166, 196, 200,
   203**
   founded by Jai Singh, 97
   heavily concentrated north
      of Amritsar, 97
   face Sukerchakia and
      Ramgarhia forces near
      Achal, 98
   with help of Ahluwalia
      chief expel Ramgarhia
      from Bist-Doab, 98

   relations between Jai Singh
      and Maha Singh curdle,
      98
   decline of Kanhaya misl,
      99
   Jai Singh distraught
      death of son, 99
   Sada Kaur takes over
      control of Kanhaya
      misl, 100
   with help from Ranjit
      Singh oust Ramgarhia
      from Batala, 109
   fading away of misl

Sada Kaur takes charge, 153

Kapur Singh, 97
  recognized leader organizes jathas, 73
  administered baptism to many inluding Ala Singh, 112
  godfather to Jassa Singh Ahluwalia, 113
  appointed commander of Budha Dal in 1733, 113
  bestowed title of nawab, 187
  hold Lahore at their mercy, 193

Karam Singh
  becomes leader of Shaheedan misl, 123
  distinguished himself at the battle of Jalalabad, 123
  succeeds Sahib Singh as head of Phulkian, loyal to the British, 142

Karorasinghian, 115
  founded by Karori Mal, 115
  attacks Phulkian misldar near Ghurram a truce, 117
  Jodh Singh takes control of misl, 119

Kaura Mal, 104, 190
  appointed Diwan of Multan, 192

Khalsa
  a diversity of practices, 55

Kharak Singh
  ascends throne in 1839, 102

Khushal Singh, 103

Kiratpur
  a safe haven, 25

Lakhpat Rai
  Diwan of Lahore province, 74
  vowed to eliminate Singhs, 74

Lehna Singh, 86, 87, 94, 200

Madho Das
  receives baptism and takes name Banda Singh, 47

Maha Singh
  lays siege of Sodhra fort, 93
  a scion of Sukerchakia misldar, 98
  relations with Kanhaya misldar curdle, 98
  seeks help of Ramgarhia chief against Kanhaya misldar, 98
  suffers defeat at Naushera and retreats to Nurpur, 99
  refuses to share spoils with Sukerchakia sardar, 106
  lures Ramgarhia misl to join forces against Kanhaya misl, 109
  plans to recover zamzama gun from Pir Mahomed, 149
  assisted by Kanhaya misldar lay siege of Rassulnagar, a Chatthas fortress, 149
  on mission to subdue all other misls, 150

falling-out with Kanhaya misldar
battle of Batala, 152
incensed by humiliation, 152
alleged matricide, 167
suffers defeat in Jammu, 152

Maharaja Ranjit Singh
the extent of empire, 17

Mali Singh
Ramgarhia sibling skirmishes with Ahluwalia chieftain, 107

Malwa
tribal groups, 16

Manoo Mall, 137, 139

Marathas
a militarized people, 175
first people to challenge Muslim rule, 176
Shahu becomes overlord of the people appoints Balaji peshwa, 177
quid pro quo for help Moguls grant governance of Deccan, 179
In 1720 Baji Rao confirmed Peshwa felt it time to end Mogul rule, 180
internecine warfare, 182
General Raghunath Rao captures Delhi in 1757, 183
overran Punjab establish garrison at Lahore, 184
Afghans end Maratha hegemony over Punjab battle of Panipat, 186

Mata Sundri
overture by Mogul emperor, 65
dismayed by infighting ng between Tat Khlasa and Bandais, 72
takes child Jassa Singh Ahluwalia under her wing, 127

Mehar Singh
died in battle with ruler of Murinda, 124
takes control of Nishanwalia misl, 124

Mir Mannu, 104, 191, 193
son of Qamaruddin Khan, 192
sues for peace and becomes an Afghan feudatory, 193

Misls
Bhangi, 86
Kanhaya, 97
Ramgarhia, 103
Singhapuria, 112
Karorasinghian, 115
Nakkai, 120
Dallewalian, 120
Shaheedan, 122
Nishanwalia, 123
Ahluwalia, 126
Phulkian, 132
Sukerchakia, 144
thrive on pillage, 79
leaders carve spheres of control, 80

the ebb and flow of misl
hegemony, 81
hankered to wrest control
of Lahore, 83
Mogul
appeal to key Muslim
groups, 54
resolve to annihilate Sikhs,
57
imperial forces pursue
Banda Bahadur, 58
Emperor Shah Alam ll
negotiates treaty with
Sikhs, 117
facing threats from East
India company, the
Marathas and Sikhs,
117
heir apparents served in
the Deccan, 175
shed Turkic and adopt
Persian language, 189
Nadir Shah
invades India in 1739
defeats Mogul at Battle
of Karnal, 188
Nakkai
Chieftain Gyan Singh has
his sister Raj Kaur to
marry Ranjit Singh
offspring Kharak Singh,
120
founded by Hira Singh,
120
internecine feud, 120, 121
Nand Singh
appoints Jassa Singh
Ramgarhia as militia
commander, 103

Nijab-ul- Daula, governor of Saharanpur., 116
Nishanwalia
founded by Dasaunda
Singh, 123
Ranjit Singh ceded control
to Daya Kaur, 123
Nodh Singh
a feared leader, marries a
Majithia girl, 146
came to be known as chief
of Sukerchak, 146
Obed Khan, 196
Panth
divided into Tat Khalsa
and Bandais, 72
forgives Jassa Singh
Ramgarhia
fort renamed Ramgarh,
105
Phul
belonged to Siddhu jat
tribe, 132
thirtieth in descent from
Raja Jaisal, 132
grandfather to Ala Singh,
133
Phulkian, 77, 78, 88, 112, 116, 130, 132, 134, 135, 138, 140, 142, 171, 201, 203, 213
Ala Singh a proxy for
Abdali, 88
Paur progenitor of Patiala,
Nabha and Jind rulers,
132

founded by Phul, 132
only misl not part of Dal
   Khalsa, 133
policy of survival, 134
did not come to the aid of
   women fleeing Abdali
   vada Ghallughara, 135
war of succession
   Amar Singh prevails,
   135
succored Abdali in 1767
   awarded Sirhind, 136
infighting over regency,
   138
Sahib Kaur made wazir
   repels Marathas, 139
seek British protection, 141
stood by British during
   1857 mutiny
   awarded jagirs, 143
sycophant of Abdali
   outraged Dal Khalsa,
   147

Punjab
a sacred ground, 12
spiritual center of the
   Sikhs, 12
Alexander the Great, 12
invaded and pillaged, 12
divided into Doabs, 13
land of five rivers, 13
partitioned in 1947, 17
a scattering of villages, 50
Lahore and Multan two
   major cities, 51
a prized possession of
   Moguls, 189
Lahore most coveted, 190
a privileged appointment
   for nobles, 190
a Mogul in-house
   imbroglio, 194

Qamaruddin Khan,
190, 191
Mogul wazir, 192

Raja Ajmer Chand
attacks Anandpur Sahib in
   1703, 38
seeks help of Aurengzeb,
   38

Raja Bhim Chand
chief of Bilaspur, 32

Raja Medini Prakash
lord of Paonta Sahib, 32

Raja Rawal Jaisal
a Bhatti Rajput and
   Phulkian progenitor,
   132

Ram Rauni, 104, 194

Ramgarhia, 77, 83, 90,
91, 96, 98, 103, 104,
106, 107, 129, 152,
158, 160, 164, 165,
194, 200
a renamed misl, 103
feud with Kanhaya over
   sharing of revenues,
   105
most of time in feud with
   Kanhayia and
   Ahluwalia misldars, 105
dislodged by Kanhaya misl,
   106
relations with Ahluwalia
   soured after battle of
   Dina Nagar, 107
lured by Maha Singh to
   join forces against
   Kanhaya misl, 109
prevail in Batala, 109

feud between heirs
prompts Ranjit Singh to
appropriate all of their
territories, 110

Ran Singh
extnded widely Nakkai
misl's sphere of control,
121

**Rani Rajindar Kaur,
138**

**Ranjit Singh, 16, 17,
91, 94, 96, 100, 101,
109, 110, 114, 118,
120, 121, 125, 131,
142, 153, 154, 157,
158, 161, 165, 167,
170, 204**
succeeds Maha Singh, 153
little schooling but a beau
ideal soldier, 155
kills his mother, 156
captures Lahore, 158
dislodges Bhangi misldar
and captures Amritsar,
159
proclaimed Maharaja in
1801, 159
no designs on Ahluwalia
territories, 160
ambitions to conquer
Malwa thwarted, 161
held Ahluwalia chief in
high esteem, 167
concedes his rule not
extend beyond Sutlej
River, 170
pleads with fellow misldars
for a unified alliance,
203

**Sada Kaur, 95, 100,
109, 153, 155, 158,
165, 167, 203**
helps Ranjit Singh launch
attack on Lahore, 95
gets her daughter
betrothed to Ranjit
Singh, 100
takes control of Kanhaya
misl, 100
seeks to elevate grandson
Sher Singh as next in
line to Sukerchakia
throne, 101
enraged Kharak Singh
cosen as heir
conspires with the
British, 101
harassed by Ramgarhia
appeals to Ranjit Singh,
109
a ladder for Ranjit Singh to
reach the summit of
power, 168
chides misldars for not
being man enough, 203

Sadhu Singh
great grandson Badar Singh
marries a kala girl, 126
raised in maternal vaillage
of Kalal, 126
vowed progeny will
exclusively marry into
kalal family, 126

Sahib Kaur
elder sister to Sahib Singh,
Phulkian misldar, 137
appointed wazir, 139
routs Marathas, 140

taken into custody by brother Sahib Singh, 140
Sahib Singh, 91, 93
a debauchee and drunkard, 94
Sangat Singh, 124
Sarbat Khalsa
Baisakhi 1748 merge jaths into misls, 76
resolve to rerake Lahore, 200
Shah Jahan
crowned emperor, 24
Shah Nawaz
invites Ahmade Shah Abdali to invade India, 75
Shaheedan
battle of Goharwal, Baba Deep Singh martyred, 122
founded by Baba Deep Singh, 122
Sikhs
spot Jassa Singh Ramgarhia among enemy, 104
trapped in fort at Ram Rauni, 104
hunted down by Moguls, 194
inflict heavy losses on Moguls, 197
take control of territory from Sutlej to the Indus, 198
clobber the Afghans, 199
misldars promote Khalsa creed, 211
no evidence of engaging in battle with Abdali, 211
Singhpuria
also known as Fyzulpuria misl
founded by Kapur Singh, 112
Sukerchakia, 77, 79, 87, 89, 91, 93, 95, 98, 99, 101, 109, 121, 144, 147, 149, 152, 154, 164, 168, 196, 199, 203, 207

misldar Charhat Singh dies accidentally, 89
Ranjit Singh and Ahluwalia chied attack Bhangi fort in 1804, 92
descendent Kiddoh relocates to Sukerchak in 1555, 144
leaders known for courage and guile, 144
lineal descent from Kalu connection to sansi tribe, 144
Ranjit Singh succeeds Maha Singh, 153
internecine warfare, 164
assisted by Kanhaya misl force Ramgarhia to flee to Hissar, 165
help Sada Kaur to force Ramgarhias to vacate Punjab, 165
Charhat Singh emerges leader, 196
Tara Singh Gaibe

Ramgarhia sibling killed in battle, 108
Dallewalian misldar, 115
earned his name Gheba, 120

Tegh Bahadur
ascension to guruship, 27

Yahya Khan, 74, 75, 191, 192

Zahura
Ahluwalia and Ramgarhia fight pitched battle, 129

Zakaria Khan, 187, 190, 192
Governor of Lahore, 187
dies in 1745, 191

Zaman Shah Durrani
son of Timur invades India in 1796, 157

Bhupinder Singh Mahal has written extensively for Sikh journals, newspapers and magazines in Canada, United States, England and India on Sikh ethos in general and evolving situations and challenges facing Sikh Diaspora in particular.

He has lived and or worked on five continents. His international manifold experience has provided him with a platform to promote multiculturalism in Canada. From 1990 to 1994 he served on the Canadian Multiculturalism Advisory Committee, a body responsible for policy development in the elimination of barriers to achieve social, cultural and economic equality for all Canadians.

Since 1997 he has been playing a very proactive role in the health care arena: serving four years as Vice Chair of a leading health provider organization and by serving on the Council of the College of Physiotherapists, both Order-in-Council appointments by the Ontario government.

In March 2009 Mr. Mahal was appointed Chairperson, Employment Insurance Board of Referees (a Governor-in-Council appointment). The legislatively prescribed Board is a first-level, independent, administrative tribunal mandated to provide fair and impartial quasi-judicial hearings of appeals of Employment Insurance decisions.

In 2003 he was awarded the Queen's Golden Jubilee Medal for contributions to Canada and to fellow Canadians. In 2007 he was awarded Council Award by the College of Physiotherapists of Ontario in recognition of significant contributions ensuring the physiotherapists provide high quality, competent and ethical services that protect the public interest.